T0317785

LONDON TUBE STATIONS

1924–1961

PHOTOGRAPHS

PHILIP BUTLER

TEXT

JOSHUA ABBOTT

FUEL

CONTENTS

6 FOREWORD : THE ALLURE OF THE SUBTERRANEAN

10 INTRODUCTION : MEDIEVAL MODERNISM

22 A NEW BEGINNING : THE NORTHERN LINE EXTENSION TO MORDEN 1924-1926

40 RE-MAKE, RE-MODEL : THE CENTRAL LONDON STATIONS 1927-1935

58 LITTLE BOXES : THE PICCADILLY LINE WEST 1931-1934

80 INTO NEW COUNTRY : THE PICCADILLY LINE EAST 1932-1933

98 REPEAT PERFORMANCE : THE DISTRICT LINE EAST 1932-1935

108 FIVE-YEAR PLAN : THE NEW WORKS PROGRAMME 1935-1939

130 BEFORE THE JUBILEE : THE BAKERLOO LINE NORTH 1936-1939

144 BRANCHING OUT : THE CENTRAL LINE EAST 1940-1948

168 THE LONG GOODBYE : THE CENTRAL LINE WEST 1940-1961

190 VICTIMS OF PROGRESS : DEMOLISHED STATIONS

196 INDEX OF STATIONS

198 BIBLIOGRAPHY

199 BIOGRAPHIES

Northfields Depot

FOREWORD : THE ALLURE OF THE SUBTERRANEAN

Is there anything more enticing on a rainy London evening than the glow of an Underground station? The luminous red lollipop roundel invites the weary pedestrian to enter and be whisked away on a clanking, disorientating journey under the metropolis, eventually emerging at one of the sister stations, miles from the point of departure.

I've nursed a long-standing fascination for the Underground since childhood. Regular day trips from my family home on the south coast to the capital were always anticipated with fevered delight, especially the prospect of descending into the depths to ride the tube. The whirring escalators, sudden gusts of air, moquette seats, tile patterns, and those funny balls hanging from the carriage ceilings all transfixed me and cemented the tube in my subconscious as a curious and enthralling place. As I grew older, I began to pay more attention to the stations themselves, appreciating both the forms and decorative details that are so unique to the network.

The London Underground currently has 272 stations, and while admittedly, all are on equal footing when functioning as portals to the trains, to me, they don't all deliver on the same emotional level. Those from the last 30 years feel efficient, occasionally impressive, but often vacuous and sterile. The early examples are charming in a heritage railway vernacular, but it's those from the 1930s that tick all the right boxes as far as I'm concerned. They are now, as they were when first constructed, unique on the streets of London. A cubist family of structures that feel simultaneously historical and futuristic.

Frank Pick, head of the Underground Electric Railways of London group during the interwar period, was well aware they were breaking new ground on these shores at the time. Britain had been slow to embrace the Modernist architecture that had swept through Europe in the 1920s, but by the early 1930s, we were being dragged into the modern age, and with the assistance of architect Charles Holden, the UERL were at the forefront of the movement.

In 1932 the UERL produced a film documenting the new Piccadilly Line extensions entitled *London's Latest Tube Railway*. Commissioned for an exhibition at Charing Cross station to showcase this latest expansion, the grainy silent footage is a fascinating window into a period of bold innovation.

UNDERGROUND

Commencing at Acton Town, we take in the crisp angular forms of brick, glass and concrete before riding the rails to visit the box-like Sudbury Town and the circular Arnos Grove. On route, we witness excavation and construction, trains running through tunnels being assembled overhead, and scores of suited onlookers marvelling at the bold new visions before their eyes.

It wasn't purely the architecture that was fresh and new at the time, though. A synchronised revamp spearheaded by Pick saw striking Art Moderne posters champion the network, a new schematic map improve the clarity of routes, and state of the art '38 rolling stock increase capacity. The whole package would transform the perception of the tube from the murky claustrophobic experience of its early years to an efficient modern system suitable for 'the machine age'.

It is with all this in mind that I embarked on this photographic project. I aimed to capture each station designed and built during this innovative period in its best light. To showcase their street-facing 'typology' and give a flavour of interior features and the general atmosphere of these iconic stations in the 21st century. Guided by Joshua's detailed overview, I hope this book proves both informative and enjoyable, highlighting just how bold this period of station design was and will perhaps bring to light some of the lesser-known examples on the far reaches of the network.

PHILIP BUTLER

Top: Loughton station; Harold Stabler tile

55 BROADWAY

OAKWOOD

N3

BARCLAYS
BANK
UNDERGROUND
STOCKWELL
STATION
STOCKWELL STATION
BANK
WALTON'S
FRUIT.
ABDULLA
F. HUDSON
CIGARS
TOBACCOS
FREQUENT
ELECTRIC
TRAINS TO
ALL PARTS
OF LONDON
BIRD'S
CUSTARD

INTRODUCTION : MEDIEVAL MODERNISM

Charles Holden's designs for the Underground from the mid-1920s to the outbreak of World War II represents a high point of transport architecture and Modernist design in Britain. His collaboration with Frank Pick, the Chief Executive of London Transport, brought about a marriage of form and function, civic service and commerce that revolutionised both the Underground brand and services offered by it. Indeed, this feat was not accomplished by the two men alone but by a host of architects, designers, builders, engineers, artists, tradespeople and bureaucrats. This army of people, working under Holden and Pick, created what Pick would term 'Medieval Modernism', comparing the extension of the Underground network to the creation of a great cathedral, many hands and years in the making. Holden's stations would also prove to have a far-reaching influence that stretched well beyond London's boundaries. As famed architectural historian Nikolaus Pevsner later noted, they would 'pave the way for the twentieth-century style in England'.

Holden and Pick weren't the first architect and management pairing to champion a distinctive identifiable design for London's Underground railway. What we now see as a unified network was originally a collection of competing companies with different designers. In the early 1900s, financier Charles Yerkes and architect Leslie Green sought to resolve this disparate approach. They introduced a standard station design for the UERL, featuring distinctive red exterior tiling, steel frame construction, and platform-level patterned tiles. Unfortunately, the early deaths of both Yerkes and Green led to financial problems and a loss of design focus that wasn't remedied until Pick met Holden in 1915 at a Design and Industries Association conference. Their subsequent collaboration would have a profound and long-lasting effect on the visual identity of the London transport network that is still felt to this day.

Charles Holden, c.1930

Charles Henry Holden was born in Great Lever, a suburb of Bolton, on 12 May 1875, the fifth child of Joseph and Ellen Holden. Charles had a disrupted childhood, his father going bankrupt when he was nine and his mother dying when he was 15. He began working at age 16 as an assistant to a surveyor and eventually became an apprentice to a Manchester architect. Relocating to London, Holden worked with architect CR Ashbee from 1897 before moving on to the practice of H Percy Adams two years later. Adams specialised in hospitals, with Holden designing several of them, such as the former children's hospital in Belgravia. Between the turn of the

Stockwell station, c.1920

century and the 1920s, Holden designed a variety of other buildings, including libraries, schools and houses. He became a partner in 1907, and when Lionel Pearson also became one in 1913, the practice was renamed Adams, Holden & Pearson. During World War I, Charles served in the Red Cross's London Ambulance Column as a stretcher-bearer, transferring wounded soldiers from stations to hospitals. In the following years, he worked for the Imperial War Graves Commission, designing cemeteries and memorials for his fallen countrymen.

Frank Pick was born in Spalding, Lincolnshire, on 23 November 1878, to Francis and Fanny Pick. After finishing his schooling, he studied law at the University of London before working for North Eastern Railways. There he became assistant to Managing Director George Gibb, and when Gibb moved to work for the Underground Electric Railways of London in 1906, Pick followed. Starting as Gibb's assistant, by 1908 Frank had become Publicity Officer, and by 1909 Traffic Development Officer. Three years later, he was the UERL's Commercial Manager. It was in this role that he started to have a visible impact on the identity of the Underground network.

Frank Pick, 1922

Pick wanted to revolutionise design on the Underground, bringing in a new eye-catching, Modernist-influenced look that would take in everything from station design to advertising to platform lighting. Pick commissioned Edward Johnston to produce his now-iconic typeface for use on all Underground materials and redesign the roundel symbol, Harry Beck to create his revolutionary tube map, and he saw Holden as the man to modernise the design of the stations.

The UERL already had a chief architect, Stanley Heaps, but Pick felt his designs were not modern enough.

Heaps had been assistant to Leslie Green and took over his role after he died of a heart attack in 1908. The first stations Heaps designed by himself followed the same approach, adopting Green's distinctive oxblood tiling and semi-circular windows. His next major set, for the expansion of the Charing Cross, Euston and Hampstead Railway (now part of the Northern Line), took a different approach. To fit in with the leafy north London suburbs, Heaps, with assistant Thomas Bilbow, designed the stations in a more suburban-style, with tiled roofs and brick colonnades. However, Pick wasn't a fan of this aesthetic and brought in Holden for the southern end of the line. Holden had previously worked on two new entrances for Westminster station (1922–4). Both were simple designs, replacing drab doorways with light and modern alternatives, a first step in dragging the tube out of the Edwardian era. His stations for the Northern Line took the next step and introduced a new style for the Underground, featuring double-height ticket halls clad in Portland stone.

Cockfosters station, 1933

B
02
STH HARROW

UNDERGROUND
UNDERGROUND

A full-scale timber and paper mock-up of proposed Northern Line stations design concept, 1925

Holden's following two projects for the UERL would become some of his most revered and would set the scene for the next few years of innovation. In 1928 he undertook the rebuilding of Piccadilly Circus station, a challenging project completed with aplomb. A subterranean elliptical ticket hall was created, clad in marble and adorned with a mural by artist Stephen Bone. The finished station was a great success, praised by the public and press alike, and moving architect Erich Mendelsohn to send Holden a postcard reading 'Wishing you many more Piccadilly Circuses'. It also would prove to be highly influential, inspiring the design of the Moscow Metro that opened seven years later.

Piccadilly Circus was swiftly followed with the substantial new headquarters for the UERL at 55 Broadway, a project that replaced the company's hodgepodge of offices in the same area. The gleaming white 14-storey building – the tallest office block in London – was labelled the city's first skyscraper and brought to mind a cathedral, proclaiming the might of the growing, centralised transport network.

In June and July 1930, Holden and Pick took a tour of Europe to explore the new Modernist architecture of the continent. They travelled through Germany, the Netherlands, Denmark and Sweden, visiting designs by the likes of Willem Dudok, with whom Pick was particularly taken. The buildings they saw eschewed decoration and concentrated on letting the function guide its form. Both men were also impressed with the use of external illuminations after dark, something they would replicate on many Underground stations. It's worth noting that they didn't visit the buildings of Le Corbusier, nor those that came out of the Bauhaus; Holden and Pick were both of a mind that exposed concrete was not appropriate for Britain, both practically or emotionally. They were determined to use what they saw as more suitable materials, primarily brick, but also wood and metal, in a bid to make the new station architecture forward-looking yet humane.

The first fruits of the European trip was the new stations designed for the Piccadilly Line at the start of the 1930s. The changes were significant, as can be seen at Sudbury Town from 1931. The Portland stone finish was replaced by locally produced brick, the three-screen facade jettisoned for a rectangular box with a focus on interior illumination, mixing natural and artificial sources. This design would provide the blueprint for the rest of the decade. The extension of the Piccadilly Line into the growing suburbs around London provided space for Holden and Pick to bring to fruition their ideal of an integrated transport network that balanced beauty and utility.

The apex of the working relationship between the two men were the new stations between Manor House and Cockfosters, lauded both in the architectural press and the network's publicity posters. The commission was given to Holden in April 1931, with the first set of stations opening the following year. Simultaneously, several new stations at the western end of the Piccadilly Line were also being built. This was a heavy workload for a relatively small firm like Adams, Holden & Pearson, so a 'one man, one station' design policy was developed. This gave Holden overall responsibility for the design concept, often producing an initial sketch, which was then worked up into a detailed plan by his assistant or the office of Stanley Heaps. Once a committee headed by Pick gave it the green light, the design was taken up by an assistant who would see it through to completion.

This method worked well through the early 1930s, but the Golden Age didn't last forever. As the 'New Works Programme' was launched in 1935 to replace older stations with the new modern London Transport style, Holden's attention and energies were being drawn to the rebuilding of the University of London in Bloomsbury, a project that would be only partially completed. The slack was taken up by the office of Stanley Heaps and a few different outside architects, like RH Uren and Leonard Bucknell, but the designs produced by this group fell below the high standards that had previously been set. Pick asked Holden to return and oversee some of the new designs, but the genie could not be put back in the bottle.

The last major project of the Pick era was the Central Line extensions on either side of London. While the plan seemed to be a rerun of the Piccadilly Line expansion of 1931–4, which set such high standards and stamped the Underground's brand on the new suburbs, the same heights could not be reached this time. War intervened, and all the designs made in the late 1930s were revised due to material and capital shortages. The eastern branch of the extension included Holden's final three stations for the network, but these would also feel the bite of austerity when construction resumed after the war. Some of the post-war redesigns were later revised even further as architectural fashion changed towards the more austere, with some stations not being completed until the early 1960s.

Pick retired from the board in 1940 after a reorganisation of the management structure. His dynamism was directed into the war effort as Director-General of the Ministry of Information, but he didn't have the same effect there as he had at London Transport, moving to the Ministry of Transport after only four months. Pick had been in poor health for a number of years, and his travels around the country for the Ministry of Transport exacerbated it. He died at his home in Golders Green on 7 November 1941.

Southgate station, bus interchange and

During the war, Holden helped draw up plans to rebuild cities damaged by the Luftwaffe. He spent the post-war years acting as a consultant to various authorities and bodies, gradually reducing his workload. He died on 1 May 1960, with his ashes spread at the Friends Meeting House in Hertford.

Despite going out with a whimper rather than a bang, the influence of the early Holden–Pick years was widespread and somewhat overbearing for those that followed. It is notable that the 1950s and 1960s produced very little in terms of new station buildings, and those that were built turned away from the 'Sudbury Box' ideal. It was not until the Jubilee Line extension of 1999 that a set of stations was produced that could take on the 1930s designs for architectural significance.

Even during the period, Holden's designs' influence was felt across the transport networks. The new stations of Southern Railway under John Robb Scott turned away from the Beaux-Arts of the 1920s towards a Modernist-influenced look, as seen at Woking, Surbiton and Bishopstone. Wallis, Gilbert & Partners, well known for their extravagant Art Deco factories, produced several Holdenesque bus garages for London Transport that eschewed the Egyptian and Aztec decorations of their industrial buildings in favour of a simpler style in detailed brickwork. The Upminster branch of the District Railway also followed the trend. Seven new station buildings by the London, Midland and Scottish Railway company's chief architect William H Hamlyn were designed in a Holden-derived brick idiom, but they lacked the lightness of touch seen in the genuine article.

Most of Charles Holden's stations are now listed by English Heritage, hopefully protecting them against demolition and disfigurement. But perhaps the biggest compliment that can be paid is the fact that they are still in use, helping millions of Londoners travel around the capital nearly 100 years after they were built. The little boxes designed by Holden to facilitate passengers' journeys have become instantly recognisable icons of London and its suburbs.

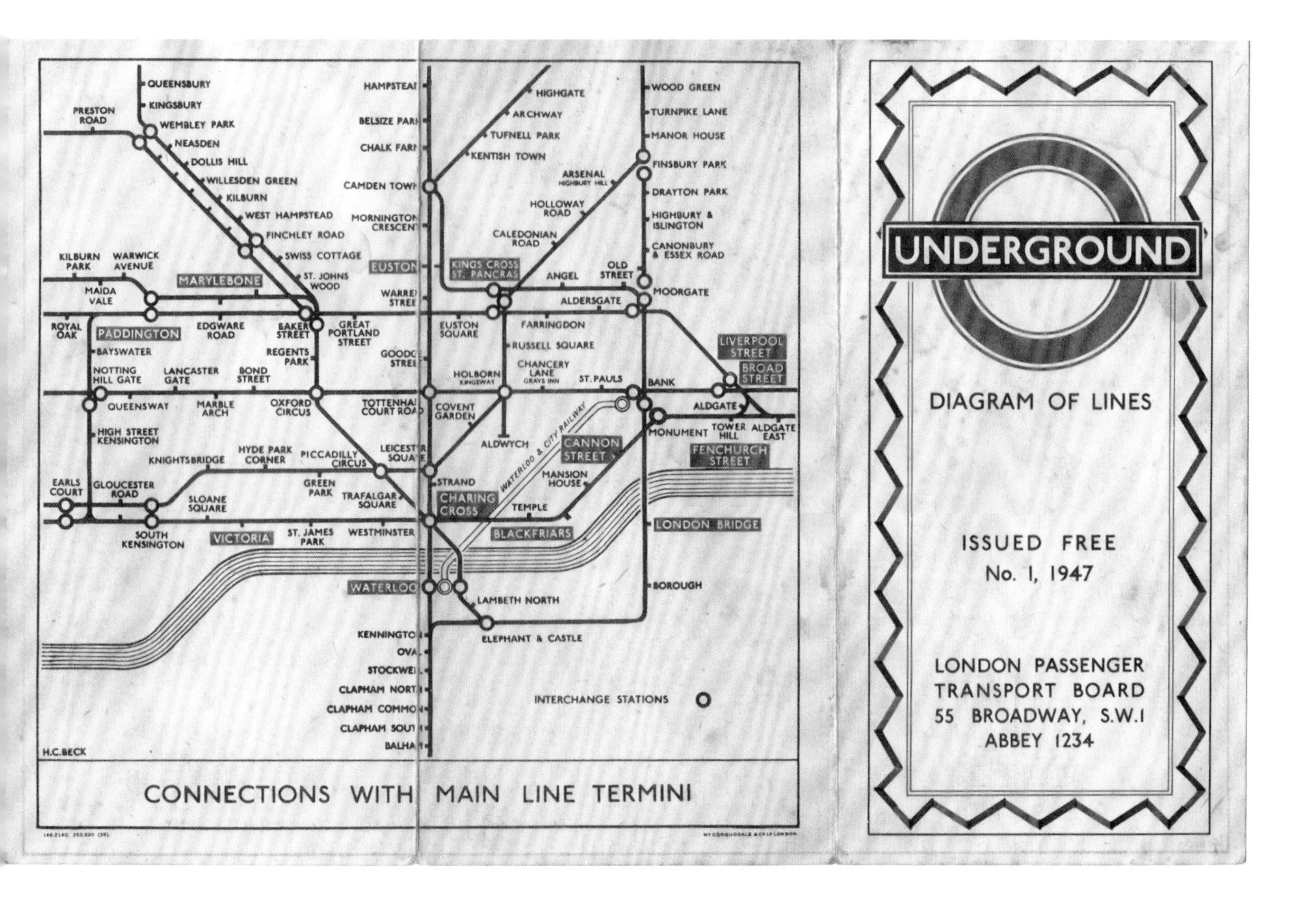
QUEENSBURY
KINGSBURY
PRESTON ROAD
WEMBLEY PARK
NEASDEN
DOLLIS HILL
WILLESDEN GREEN
KILBURN
WEST HAMPSTEAD
FINCHLEY ROAD
SWISS COTTAGE
ST. JOHNS WOOD
KILBURN PARK
WARWICK AVENUE
MARYLEBONE
MAIDA VALE
ROYAL OAK
PADDINGTON
EDGWARE ROAD
BAKER STREET
GREAT PORTLAND STREET
BAYSWATER
REGENTS PARK
NOTTING HILL GATE
LANCASTER GATE
BOND STREET
QUEENSWAY
MARBLE ARCH
OXFORD CIRCUS
HIGH STREET KENSINGTON
KNIGHTSBRIDGE
HYDE PARK CORNER
PICCADILLY CIRCUS
EARLS COURT
GLOUCESTER ROAD
GREEN PARK
TRAFALGAR SQUARE
SLOANE SQUARE
SOUTH KENSINGTON
VICTORIA
ST. JAMES PARK
WESTMINSTER
BELSIZE PARK
CHALK FARM
CAMDEN TOWN
MORNINGTON CRESCENT
EUSTON
HIGHGATE
ARCHWAY
TUFNELL PARK
KENTISH TOWN
ARSENAL
HIGHBURY HILL
HOLLOWAY ROAD
CALEDONIAN ROAD
KINGS CROSS ST. PANCRAS
ANGEL
OLD STREET
ALDERSGATE
EUSTON SQUARE
FARRINGDON
RUSSELL SQUARE
HOLBORN
KINGSWAY
CHANCERY LANE
GRAYS INN
ST. PAULS
COVENT GARDEN
ALDWYCH
WATERLOO & CITY RAILWAY
STRAND
CHARING CROSS
TEMPLE
BLACKFRIARS
CANNON STREET
MANSION HOUSE
WOOD GREEN
TURNPIKE LANE
MANOR HOUSE
FINSBURY PARK
DRAYTON PARK
HIGHBURY & ISLINGTON
CANONBURY & ESSEX ROAD
MOORGATE
LIVERPOOL STREET
BROAD STREET
BANK
ALDGATE
MONUMENT
TOWER HILL
ALDGATE EAST
FENCHURCH STREET
LONDON BRIDGE
BOROUGH
LAMBETH NORTH
ELEPHANT & CASTLE
CLAPHAM NORTH
INTERCHANGE STATIONS
H.C.BECK
CONNECTIONS WITH MAIN LINE TERMINI
UNDERGROUND
DIAGRAM OF LINES
ISSUED FREE
No. 1, 1947
LONDON PASSENGER
TRANSPORT BOARD
55 BROADWAY, S.W.1
ABBEY 1234

TO TRAINS

PLEASE WAIT IN THIS
AREA UNTIL PLATFORM
IS INDICATED
PLATFORM 3
2 PLATFORM 1
1 Uxbridge Plat 1 2 mins
No Smoking
09:14:07
1 Uxbridge Plat 1 2 mins
No Smoking
09:14:07
Please remain in this
area until platform
is indicated
Piccadilly line
← Platforms 3 and 4
Platforms 1 and 2 →

UNDERGROUND

A NEW BEGINNING : THE NORTHERN LINE EXTENSION TO MORDEN 1924–1926

The Northern Line extension stations from Clapham South to Morden were Charles Holden's first complete set of buildings for the UERL. However, these were preceded by a commission redesigning the facades of several stations on what was then the City and South London Railway. He modernised the street-level buildings at seven stations between Angel and Clapham North with new light-coloured faience tiling and a metal canopy featuring the diamond motif and the distinctive 'UNDERGROUNDD' signage. New lifts were also added, giving the service a new sense of dynamism. The eighth and only surviving example of this early work is the surface building at Clapham Common, a Neo-Classical design with little indication of what was to follow. As became the modus operandi for the next 15 years, the initial sketches were produced by Holden and implemented by Stanley Heaps and his office. However, these early revamps were dictated by the original station footprint and didn't allow Holden to stretch his wings fully.

Heaps was initially given the brief for the seven new stations from Clapham South to Morden. He had previously designed the extension stations at the other end of the line, from Brent Cross to Edgware in 1923–4, and had used a suburban villa style to harmonise with the new northern suburbs. However, the Neo-Georgian tiled roofs, brick columns and chequerboard interior floors were not what Pick had in mind for his modernisation drive – he wanted the new buildings to stand out from their neighbours, not blend in with them.

Holden followed the lead of Leslie Green, the prolific designer of stations for the UERL at the start of the century, and produced a facade that could be implemented and adapted for different sites and locations. The design could fit into an existing street parade or be used as a standalone building. This new look added space and light to the cramped, gloomy stations the public may have had in mind when visualising the Underground. The ticket halls had double-height ceilings, with light entering through large windows. The exteriors were built in Portland stone, a material lighter in tone than previous stations' terracotta tile or brick. The facades were divided into three sections or 'screens', which could be either arranged flatly or folded depending on the station's location. The designs were well received by Pick and, when built, by the architectural press too. They represented Holden's first leap forward in revolutionising the Underground, but not his last.

Entrance hall at Tooting Bec station

CLAPHAM COMMON

Clapham Common is an atypical design by Holden, who added a new entrance in 1924. The station had opened in 1900 and was the terminus of the City and South London Railway until the 1926 extension. The new building added by Holden is very much in keeping with the style of transport design of the early 20th century in the capital, influenced by Art Nouveau but with a distinctively more sombre atmosphere than the earlier Leslie Green stations. The Portland stone street-level building has a small dome with entrances on either side. Below ground, the ticket hall, corridors and platforms are lined with white, green and maroon tiles. Along with Clapham North, this station has the only central island platform, leaving little space for passengers.

Station building: 1924

Designed by: Charles Holden

Listed: Grade II

UNDERGROUND
UNDERGROUND
UNDERGROUND
UNDERGROUND
CLAPHAM
COMMON
STATION
BEERS
SODA

CLAPHAM SOUTH

Clapham South occupies a corner site with three entrances allowing easy access to passengers. The facade screen is folded around this corner, with a shop parade extending down the street. Above the station is Westbury Court, an apartment block designed by Edmund Cavanagh, added in 1934. The Morden extension stations were intended to be built on, where possible, to increase revenue for the company. Inside is a spacious ticket hall, top-lit by octagonal skylights. The platform areas retain their original tiling pattern, a pre-Holden design, with white tiles bordered by green, grey and maroon. In 1940 a deep-tunnel air-raid shelter was added to the station, which is now separately Grade II listed.

Station building: 1926

Designed by: Charles Holden

Listed: Grade II

CLAPHAM SOUTH
UNDERGROUND
UNDERGROUND
UNDERGROUND

BALHAM

Balham has two station entrances facing each other across a junction. The facades are both of the 'folded' variety, with the eastern building more pronounced. Both entrances have tripartite windows with a large roundel in the central panel. The window panels are separated by tapering mullions, with rounded capitals at the pinnacles. The subterranean ticket hall leads via escalators to a concourse area between the platforms, which retains most of the original tiling. Unlike the other extension stations, Balham opened on 6 December 1926, six weeks late due to a labour dispute.

On 14 October 1940 a bomb fell on the road above the northern end of the platforms. The resulting explosion ruptured gas, sewer and water pipes, killing 68 people.

Station building: 1926

Designed by: Charles Holden

Listed: Grade II

BALHAM
UNDERGROUND
UNDERGROUND
UNDERGROUND
BALHAM
20

TOOTING BEC

Like Balham, Tooting Bec has two entrance buildings on opposite sides of a crossroads. Again, the facades of each are folded to different degrees, with the eastern block almost rectangular. The ticket hall ceiling features the stepped design seen at the other extension stations and a circular chandelier lighting feature. Holden was responsible for both the ticket hall design and the tiling and light fittings at platform level on these extension stations. The rest of the details were carried out by the office of Stanley Heaps. Holden brought in designer Harold Stabler to design the tile patterns on the platforms, something he would also do at later Piccadilly and Central Line stations.

The station first opened as Trinity Road but was renamed on 1 October 1950.

Station building: 1926

Designed by: Charles Holden

Listed: Grade II

UNDERGROUND
UNDERGROUND
UNDERGROUND
TOOTING BEC STATION
AnyHouseCleared

TOOTING BROADWAY

Tooting Broadway has a curving screen facade, which neatly turns the corner between two shopping parades, echoing the parade opposite. The area in front of the station, with a statue of Edward VII by Luis Roslyn from 1911, is a busy and popular meeting area, an early example of the civic hub idea promoted by Frank Pick. The ticket hall features the recessed ceiling skylights seen at the other extension stations and wrought-iron grilles. The upright lamps lining the escalators were replaced in the 1990s, but the passageways and platforms retain the original tiling. The platforms also feature a somewhat incongruous brass clock manufactured by the Self Winding Clock Company of New York.

Station building: 1926

Designed by: Charles Holden

Listed: Grade II

TOOTING BROADWAY
UNDERGROUND
UNDERGROUND
UNDERGROUND
UNDERGROUND
TOOTING BROADWAY STATION
PRIMARY
20
RVP
SEE IT. SAY IT. SORTED.
free cash withdrawals
free cash withdrawals

COLLIERS WOOD

Colliers Wood sits on the junction of Christchurch Road and the High Street, giving prominence to the sharp right angle of the folded screen. The ticket hall is roughly rectangular in shape, with a parade of shops along the street side. The window onto the ticket hall has a large centre section of nine vertical strips, with two extra on either side, much smaller than those seen at the preceding stations. The concrete mullions that divide the windows are topped by capitals that take the roundel's form in three-dimensional form. The platforms have the same tiling as at other Morden extension stations and large platform roundels in wood.

Station building: 1926

Designed by: Charles Holden

Listed: Grade II

COLLIERS WOOD
UNDERGROUND
UNDERGROUND
UNDERGROUND
COLLIERS WOOD STATION
Ladbrokes

SOUTH WIMBLEDON

Opening with most of the other extension stations on 13 September 1926, this station was originally called 'South Wimbledon (Merton)' on tube maps before the suffix was dropped by 1951. The facade curves around its corner site, with three equally sized windows onto the ticket hall, and a coloured roundel in the centre. Inside the ticket hall hangs an ironwork Art Deco chandelier, as well as original light fittings fixed to the walls. There are also kiosks in the interior of the station, with wooden fixtures and fittings. The entranceways to the platforms were rebuilt in the 1990s and new tiles added to blend in with the original pattern.

Station building: 1926

Designed by: Charles Holden

Listed: Grade II

SOUTH WIMBLEDON
UNDERGROUND
UNDERGROUND
UNDERGROUND
SOUTH WIMBLEDON STATION
MAYOR OF LONDON
MORDEN
ROAD

MORDEN

The end of the line, Morden, is quite different to how it was when completed. A large 1960s office building now squats above and around the station and parade of shops. Here, the three-part facade screen is angled at 90 degrees to form a box, a precursor to the 'Sudbury Box' of five years later. The interior of the ticket hall is octagonal, with a large roof light above. The long shopping parade wings on either side of the entrance are protected from the elements by a canopy supported by hexagonal columns originally used for timetable information. Steel footbridges take passengers down to the platforms, which are covered by a traditional train shed structure.

Station building: 1926

Designed by: Charles Holden

OFFICES TO LET
CALL 020 8546 2166
CATTANEO
020 8546 2166
MORDEN
UNDERGROUND
MORDEN STATION
MORDEN NEWS
No parking
No parking

UNDERGROUND
UNDERGROUND
55 BROADWAY
ST. JAMES'S PARK STATION
SHOPPING AT 55 BROADWAY
SHOPPING AT 55 BROADWAY
SHOPPING AT 55 BROADWAY
BROADWAY
FREE

RE-MAKE, RE-MODEL :
THE CENTRAL LONDON STATIONS
1927–1935

Even though the Underground was focused on new suburban expansion in the 1920s and 1930s, several older stations in central London needed rebuilding or remodelling. Two of these – the remodelling of Piccadilly Circus station and the new headquarters for the UERL at 55 Broadway – would give national and international exposure to Holden and the Underground's new design focus. These projects would prove to be both architectural and engineering wonders, bringing Holden's take on Modernism to the cramped city centre.

The rebuilding and expansion of Piccadilly Circus caught the attention of the Soviet authorities, including Nikita Khrushchev, then in charge of the Moscow city authority, who were seeking to build a new underground system in the Soviet capital. A delegation visited Piccadilly Circus, and friendly relations were instigated between the Soviets and the UERL. So impressed were they, Soviet authorities bestowed Pick with an honorary badge of merit in 1932.

Holden's most significant project for the Underground, a new headquarters at 55 Broadway, followed swiftly after. The new building incorporating the existing St. James's Park station was a statement, embodying 'Modern London' and proclaiming the UERL's place at the heart of the capital in literal terms. The fresh white Portland stone helped the headquarters stand out from its grimy neighbours, with the *Observer* calling it 'The Cathedral of Modernity'.

Holden's other central London interventions were on a much smaller scale. The first building he had been involved with for the UERL was designing a new entrance at Westminster station in 1922. The Thameside entrance was shorn of the clutter of the previous incarnation, its plain stone finish a first step towards the coming revolution. A larger version of the Westminster facade was produced for West Kensington station in 1927, just before the twin peaks of Piccadilly Circus and 55 Broadway. In the 1930s, as the company spread its lines out into Metro-Land, a few other stations were also rebuilt; Warren Street (1933), Holborn (1933) and Leicester Square (1935), while Gillespie Road became Arsenal (1932).

55 Broadway / St. James's Park station

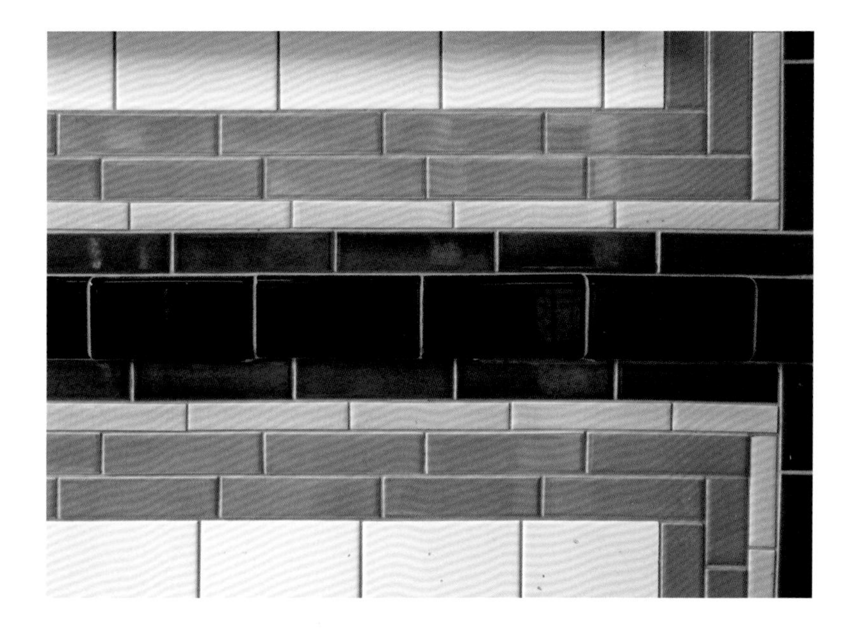

WEST KENSINGTON

Originally part of the District Railway, West Kensington opened in 1874 as 'North End (Fulham)'. It became West Kensington in 1877 and was briefly a stop on the Super Outer Circle, a short-lived line that went from Earl's Court to St. Pancras via Harlesden.

Charles Holden redesigned the street-level buildings for the station in 1927, adding a simple windowless, Portland stone facade with two entrances (one is now closed) and a roundel with central mast. The interior of the ticket hall is decorated with black, green and cream tiles, a pattern that extends down to the platforms.

Station building: 1927

Designed by: Charles Holden

UNDERGROUND
WEST KENSINGTON
SHAHIN BARBERS
BUS STOP

PICCADILLY CIRCUS

Piccadilly Circus station first opened in 1906, providing a much-needed stop in central London, with 1.5 million passengers using it in the first year. By 1922 that figure had grown to 18 million, creating the need for a new, expanded station. The location, in the middle of John Nash's circus of 1819, made large-scale building difficult. Holden's elegant solution was to bring the ticket hall underground, producing an elliptical plan that allowed passengers to circulate to and from the platforms. The new subterranean structure was built in reinforced concrete supported by seven main steel pillars and 50 smaller ones. Holden finished the ticket hall in travertine marble and bronze handrails, luxury materials not usually associated with the Underground.

Station building: 1925–8

Designed by: Charles Holden

Listed: Grade II

BEAUTY

ST. JAMES'S PARK / 55 BROADWAY

St. James's Park station had been in place since 1868, opened as part of the first section of the District Line. When the UERL decided to bring its various scattered departments under one roof, St. James's Park was their chosen location. A new building was to be constructed on top of the subterranean station, which had been remodelled a few years earlier and required minimal alteration.

An initial plan by Sir AE Richardson was deemed too old fashioned by Frank Pick, and he turned to Holden to design a building fit for the forward-looking company he wanted the UERL to become.

Station building: 1927–9

Designed by: Charles Holden

Listed: Grade I

55 BROADWAY
UNDERGROUND
ST. JAMES'S PARK STATION
PETTY FRANCE SW1
LFB

The site chosen for the building was a cramped asymmetrical plot. To counteract this, Holden arranged the building in an irregular cruciform plan, with a long east-west axis and a shorter north-south one.

It was constructed around a steel frame encased in concrete and then clad in stone – Portland from the third storey upwards, with blue-green Norwegian granite for the first and second. The upper floors step in, reducing the floor area as the building gets taller, thus maximising the amount of natural light streaming into each office and reaching street level. Services such as lifts and ventilation were built into the central tower core.

Holden commissioned seven leading British avant-garde artists to create sculptures to adorn the exterior of 55 Broadway. Reliefs depicting the Four Winds were sculpted by Eric Gill, Henry Moore, Alfred Gerrard, Eric Aumonier, Allan Wyon and Sam Rabinovitch, while Jacob Epstein designed two sculptures, *Day* and *Night*. These last two proved controversial, with the graphic nakedness of the child figure of *Day* having to be toned down.

Travertine limestone flooring forms three paved public arcades and covers the staircases, with bronze used for the railings and door furniture. Offices featured walnut doors with teak parquet, with the lower storeys possessing a slightly les lavish finish than the higher senior managemen levels. Each floor also contained a drinking fountai and an automatic mail chute; details picked up from American office designs of the time.

The Grade I listed building served as the HQ o London Transport for 90 years but was vacated i 2019 and is now being converted into a hotel.

UNDERGROUND

ARSENAL

Opened initially as Gillespie Road in December 1906 when it was part of the Great Northern, Piccadilly and Brompton Railway, the station was a typical Leslie Green design with an oxblood tiled facade. This was rebuilt and reopened in October 1932 as Arsenal (Highbury Hill), apparently at the suggestion of Arsenal's legendary manager Herbert Chapman. The suffix was dropped in the 1960s. The 1932 station design was based on a sketch by Charles Holden, which the office of Stanley Heaps enacted. The old entrance was replaced with a bold rendered facade with a giant roundel in coloured tile, prominent among the neighbouring terraced houses. The platform and connecting tunnel retain their Green-era tiles.

Station building: 1932

Designed by: Charles Holden

UNDERGROUND
ARSENAL STATION
Except
cycles
LFB
ARSENAL STATION
NO THROUGH
ROUTE
EXCEPT CYCLES

WARREN STREET

Sited on a prominent corner junction between Tottenham Court Road and Euston Road, Warren Street station is the amalgamation of three different eras. Leslie Green designed the first incarnation for the Charing Cross, Euston & Hampstead Railway in 1907. The station was slightly resited and rebuilt in 1933 when Charles Holden designed a new circular ticket hall in Portland stone, a curious mix of his previous Northern Line and Piccadilly Line designs. Like other, more central stations, the ticket hall was built upon in 1939, with a brick superstructure containing flats. The station was included in the new Victoria Line in 1968, with escalators installed and additional platforms featuring tiled artwork of a maze, or 'rabbit warren', by Crosby/Fletcher/Forbes.

Station building: 1933

Designed by: Charles Holden and Stanley Heaps

WARREN STREET STATION
WARREN STREET STATION
DRAXFLASH
Staying
home
out
Uber

HOLBORN

Like Warren Street, Holborn had originally been designed by Leslie Green, this time for the Great Northern, Piccadilly and Brompton Railway. Due to a stipulation about the architectural finishes used on Kingsway (where the main entrance faces), Green used coloured granite rather than his usual oxblood faience. Holden replaced this with a Portland stone screen, influenced by his Northern Line stations of 1926. The main entrance screen is flat with a large three-part window on the first-floor level featuring a roundel. A smaller entrance faces onto High Holborn, consisting of just one section. The platform areas were retiled in the 1980s to Roman and Egyptian inspired designs by Allan Drummond in reference to the nearby British Museum.

Station building: 1933

Designed by: Charles Holden

UNDERGROUND
UNDERGROUND
UNDERGROUND
HOLBORN STATION

LEICESTER SQUARE

Leicester Square station opened in 1906, as part of the Great Northern, Piccadilly and Brompton Railway. By the mid-1920s, an enlargement was needed to cater for the increasing popularity of the 'West End' theatre district and the new cinemas nearby. The main surface building added by Holden combines an entrance to the subsurface and pub (originally The Scotch Stores) on the junctions of Charing Cross Road and Cranbourn Street. This building revisits the earlier Northern Line aesthetic of Portland stone with a three-sided structure angling around the street corner. The platform and circulation areas were retiled in the 1980s, replacing the 1933 colour scheme of cream, blue and black tiling. A further building was designed by Holden as part of his extension, an electricity substation and pub (The Sussex), on the corner of Upper St. Martin's Lane, but that has now been redeveloped.

Station building: 1935

Designed by: Charles Holden

UNDERGROUND
CRANBOURN ST
CHARING CROSS RD
LEICESTER SQUARE STATION
LEICESTER SQUARE STATION
WYNDHAMS
ST. MARTIN'S COURT WC2
PUB&DINING

UNDERGROUND
NORTHFIELD
STATION
No parking
Offenders will be prosecuted
PAPER ONLY
Tel: 020 7918 6621
Coffee

LITTLE BOXES : THE PICCADILLY LINE WEST 1931–1934

After the success of the Northern Line extension, Piccadilly Circus, and Pick and Holden's trip to Europe, the next step was to extend the Piccadilly Line both west and east. The western branch was not as neat as the eastern, which saw eight brand new stations built. In the west, the Piccadilly Line extension replaced the existing District Railway service, which was struggling with the rapid suburban population increase of the period. The designs for the new station buildings would see the next step in Holden's quest for beauty and utility by introducing his 'Sudbury Box' model.

Holden would spend the first five years of the 1930s trying to find the best way to move passengers from platform to street level and vice versa. His quest would take in various shaped plans; rectangular, square, circular, heptagonal and even elliptical. The earliest examples are the heptagonal stations at Hounslow West and Ealing Common. These two are a step on from the Northern Line designs of 1926, turning the three-section screen facade into a stand-alone station building. Like the Northern Line buildings, they were faced with Portland stone, a half step between old-fashioned railway grandiosity and the new functionalism.

The decisive next stage of evolution would come with Sudbury Town in July 1931. Gone was any pretence to the grand station idea or the timid country halt seen more often in the western suburbs, replaced by a bold angular box. Holden succinctly described this approach as 'a brick box with a concrete lid'. Of course, this basic functionality was deliberate and the result of great thought by Holden. This form was then repeated at Acton Town, Alperton, Sudbury Hill and Northfields, as recognisable a brand as the clean facades of the Northern Line.

Holden did venture into new forms on this section of the Piccadilly Line too. Chiswick Park, not actually on the Piccadilly Line but the District, predates Holden's experiments with the circular at Arnos Grove and Southgate by a year. A couple of years later came Boston Manor and Osterley, harbingers of the billboard-style Pick wanted for the network.

Northfields station

EALING COMMON

Alongside Hounslow West, Ealing Common represents a half step from Holden, away from the more formal Northern Line station style, towards a European-influenced aesthetic. The three-screen facade has been fleshed out into a heptagonal ticket hall building, still in heavy Portland stone. Inside, the ticket hall features decorative floor tiling in the form of a star, mirroring the heptagonal drum above and on the interior walls. The platforms feature curved, cantilever platform shelters as seen at Chiswick Park and elsewhere.

The original station first opened in 1879, with the rebuilt structure opening on 1 March 1931.

Station building: 1931

Designed by: Charles Holden

UNDERGROUND
98%
EALING COMMON STATION
THE FIFTH TASTE
kworth

HOUNSLOW WEST

The new Hounslow West station opened on 5 July 1931, replacing the original District Railway station of 1884. Like Ealing Common, which had opened four months earlier, Hounslow West has a heptagonal ticket hall, clad in Portland stone. Inside hangs a bronze chandelier with seven heptagonal light fittings, echoing the plan of the ticket hall. The interior also features tiling in a cream and pink design that runs around the ticket hall's circumference. This was designed by artist Basil Ionides, known for his redesign of the Savoy Theatre and Claridge's Restaurant. The platforms were rebuilt in the mid-1970s to accommodate a rail upgrade needed for the Heathrow extension.

Station building: 1932

Designed by: Charles Holden

Listed: Grade II

UNDERGROUND
HOUNSLOW WEST STATION
PREMIUM NEWS
We Sell
Tobacco
Confectionery
Cold Drinks
Newspaper
Mobile Top-up
No parking
Offenders will be prosecuted
No parking
Offenders will be prosecuted

CHISWICK PARK

Chiswick Park was Holden's first attempt at a circular ticket hall and possibly the first indication of the influence of the new European transport architecture. The new building replaced a station from 1879 to accommodate the new Piccadilly Line track extension from Hammersmith. As became standard, the design originated with Holden and was then given over to the office of Stanley Heaps to produce the final plan. This scheme sees a semi-circular drum ticket hall sitting on a curved brick base incorporating a shopping parade. A brick tower rises beside it, emblazoned with the station name and London Transport logo. The influence of Heaps can be seen in the curved platform shelters, which were built in concrete and left unvarnished.

Station building: 1932

Designed by: Charles Holden

Listed: Grade II

UNDERGROUND
CHISWICK PARK
CHISWICK PARK STATION
BORTHWICKS

ACTON TOWN

A perfect example of the brick-box style, the current Acton Town station is the third iteration on the site since 1879. The design came from Holden via the office of Stanley Heaps, who was once again tasked with setting out the staircases and platform areas. The long side of the box faces onto Bollo Lane, with a one-storey structure containing the entrance and a shop parade. Above this rises the ticket hall, with its six vertical strip windows and overhanging concrete roof. The station was built using a mixture of prefabricated and in situ concrete construction and red brick infill. The platform level has an array of concrete features such as the two footbridges (one for staff only), the passenger shelters and a K8 phone box (again for staff use).

Station building: 1932–3

Designed by: Charles Holden

Listed: Grade II

UNDERGROUND
ACTON
TOWN
STATION
UNDERGROUND

ALPERTON

Alperton represented a design challenge for Holden and Heaps, with the railway positioned on a viaduct 30 feet above street level. Their solution was to place a rectangular ticket hall at 90 degrees to the railway, with the platform canopies joining the building's outline from the street. This elevation change necessitated a steep passenger staircase to and from the platforms. To improve access, an escalator – rehoused from the Dome of Discovery at the Festival of Britain – was installed in 1955. It is still in place but unfortunately bricked in by a wall. Next to the station is Alperton Bus Garage, designed by Stanley Heaps and opened in 1938.

Station building: 1932–3

Designed by: Charles Holden

ALPERTON STATION
UNDERGROUND
No parking

SUDBURY TOWN

Sudbury Town is the station design that provided a blueprint for Britain's next ten years of transport architecture. Stanley Heaps originally designed a heptagonal station for this plot continuing the Hounslow West concept. This was rejected, and Holden produced a simple yet radical plan, dispensing with the formality of previous designs in favour of a brick rectangle with an overhanging concrete roof. Large, vertical strip windows bring light into the three-storey brick box. Inside, the ticket hall features a newspaper kiosk and a large clock and barometer on the wall. The platform area has a curved waiting room to allow passengers sight of their train coming along the track and a concrete footbridge to the other platform.

Station building: 1932

Designed by: Charles Holden

Listed: Grade II

SUDBURY TOWN STATION
UNDERGROUND
No parking

SUDBURY HILL

A smaller but no less successful version of the 'Sudbury Box', Sudbury Hill opened a year after its bigger brother one stop away. This station has just one vertical window strip in the facade, a single-storey entrance with curved shopfronts either side. The front forecourt also features a large roundel and column projecting the Underground's branding out into the street. Behind the ticket hall is an electricity substation, hidden in a plain brick structure as a continuation of the station building. Like Sudbury Town, there is a white painted concrete footbridge across the platforms.

Station building: 1932–3

Designed by: Charles Holden

Listed: Grade II

UNDERGROUND
SU BURY HILL STATION
DRY CLEA

NORTHFIELDS

Northfields uses a 'Sudbury Box' and, unlike its brethren, turns the short face to the street. This was due to the awkward site, with the station sitting above the track. The original Edwardian station was demolished to make way for the new Northfields depot, built to house the extra trains needed for the Piccadilly Line to replace the District Railway service. The bottom half of the exterior is covered with glazed blue-black bricks, used to cut down on damage by passengers during their commute. This experiment was not repeated at any other stations. The ticket hall features a coffered ceiling and roundels in coloured glass at either end of the hall. The platform shelters are similar to those used on the eastern Piccadilly extension, with canopies inset with peaked roof windows and concrete slab name boards.

Station building: 1932

Designed by: Charles Holden

Listed: Grade II

UNDERGROUND
NORTHFIELDS STATION
No parking
Coffee 99p
No parking

BOSTON MANOR

Boston Manor and Osterley, both opened on 25 March 1934, mark a turning point away from functional design towards something more eye-catching. Frank Pick had been pushing Holden to produce station designs that would also act as billboards for the Underground's expansion into suburbia. These stations near the newly built Great West Road provided the perfect testbeds. Boston Manor replaced the 1883 station with a low building, balanced by a tall, flat tower topped with glass bricks that illuminate at night and a large roundel on a background of cream tiles. The station design, handled by Holden's assistant Charles Hutton, is clearly influenced by the Volharding building in The Hague, designed by JWE Buijs and Joan B Lursen in 1928.

Station building: 1933–4

Designed by: Charles Holden

Listed: Grade II

BOSTON MANOR STATION
JOE • COFFEE SHOP

OSTERLEY

Like Boston Manor, Osterley eschews the box-style station in favour of a squat ticket hall building with a totem-like tower topped by a concrete finial. The original design was produced by Stanley Heaps, who envisioned a box-style station. However, Frank Pick wanted something more enticing to draw in potential passengers to the station, situated alongside the busy Great West Road. As at Osterley, Charles Holden and Charles Hutton produced a new design, with a tower influenced by the Telegraaf Building in Amsterdam by JF Staaf & GJ Langhout, completed in 1930, a reminder of the importance of the 1930 European trip by Holden and Pick. The station building includes a long glazed passenger footbridge over the tracks to the eastbound platform.

Station building: 1934

Designed by: Charles Holden

Listed: Grade II

OSTERLEY STATION

2
WAY OUT
WAY OUT

INTO NEW COUNTRY : THE PICCADILLY LINE EAST 1932–1933

The Piccadilly Line extension stations to Cockfosters are probably the finest example of the collaboration between Charles Holden and Frank Pick and the most coherent set of buildings Holden produced for the tube network. Unlike earlier stations that were designed as needed, usually to replace older buildings, these eight were all built in new locations, seeking to extend London Underground's transport monopoly to the growing suburbs.

Eight stations, as well as signal boxes, electricity substations and a new depot, were designed and built between April 1931, when Holden was given the commission, and July 1933, when the last station, Cockfosters, was opened. Despite Holden having star billing, the endeavour to create this expansion was very much a team effort. Charles Holloway James designed the buildings at Bounds Green and Oakwood, although very much in the 'Sudbury Box' style. James was an architect better known for his residential work. He had previously been an assistant to Edwin Lutyens and then Raymond Unwin, working on housing in Letchworth Garden City and Hampstead Garden Suburb. Holden and James had previously designed a stand for the Empire Marketing Board at the British Industries Fair in 1931.

Other architects involved in the extension stations included Charles Hutton and Israel Schultz, both assistants at Adams, Holden & Pearson, and Stanley Heaps, the Underground's Chief Architect. The modus operandi for the extension was 'one man, one station', with Holden supplying the initial design sketch and the likes of Hutton, Schultz or James producing the finished drawings. Heaps and his office were often tasked with designing the more functional elements such as stairs and platforms.

These stations also mark the highpoint in Frank Pick's belief in the networks station being civic hubs. This meant that they were to incorporate a range of services such as shops, train information and even, in the case of Wood Green, an exhibition hall (though this was later turned into staff offices). The stations were also sited to connect with other London Transport services like bus and tram. Tram stops designed by Holden were prominent at Manor House and Turnpike Lane, before the service was axed in 1938, and the building cleared away for the extended bus routes.

Manor House aside, all of the stations on this stretch of line are Listed by Historic England, highlighting their architectural importance.

MANOR HOUSE

Manor House may be the least distinguished of the eastern Piccadilly extension stations, but it does have some interesting design details. The station is situated on a busy road junction with nine subway entrances and a modest street-level building with glass bricks. The subterranean ticket hall features a ceiling design of interlocking concentric circles and cylindrical glass timetable and fare displays units. The platforms have decorative metal ventilation grilles, designed by Harold Stabler, said to depict the myths and legends of the local area.

Station building: 1932

Designed by: Charles Holden

UNDERGROUND
Public subway
MANOR HOUSE STATION
Shop Local
Wear a mask
Save Lives
20

TURNPIKE LANE

Turnpike Lane station sits in a prominent position at the junction of Wood Green High Street, Green Lanes and Westbury Avenue. The building is square in plan, with the ticket hall floor below ground level to allow access from the various subway tunnels. The large, metal-framed windows allow light into the substantial ticket hall, illuminating the coffered ceiling. This station is an excellent illustration of the civic hub idea beloved by Frank Pick, originally integrating with a tram service (stopped in 1938) and the adjacent bus station.

Station building: 1932

Designed by: Charles Holden

Listed: Grade II

UNDERGROUND
TURNPIKE LANE
TURUL PROJECT

WOOD GREEN

Unlike the other extension stations which sit away from their neighbours, Wood Green was built into an existing parade. As a result, the station plan is an ellipse, neatly rounding the corner of the street. Although Grade II listed, many of the fixtures and fittings are replacements, a reminder of the poor condition many of these buildings fell into during the 1980s before their eventual restoration and listing. However, Harold Stabler's metalwork, including a 'Telephones' sign in the ticket hall and intricate ventilation grilles at platform level, remains.

Station building: 1932

Designed by: Charles Holden

Listed: Grade II

UNDERGROUND
UNDERGROUND
UNDERGROUND
WOOD GREEN STATION

BOUNDS GREEN

A variation on the Holden 'Sudbury Box', the ticket hall at Bounds Green features chamfered edges, allowing more daylight into the interior. The octagonal building is counterbalanced by a rectangular ventilation tower with bright blue louvres. The concourse area features two bronze uplighters, originally found at all the extension stations. In this case, one is original and one a replacement. Like Wood Green, the platform area features decorative brass ventilation grilles depicting flora and fauna. The southbound platform has a plaque commemorating 19 people killed when a Luftwaffe bomb hit the station in October 1940.

Station building: 1932

Designed by: CH James

Listed: Grade II

UNDERGROUND
UNDERGROUND
UNDERGROUND
BOUNDS GREEN
BOUNDS GREEN
20

ARNOS GROVE

Widely considered one of Holden's best designs, his station at Arnos Grove combines rationalist Northern European Modernism with an Arts and Crafts appreciation of materials. The circular drum ticket hall sits on top of a square base, both formed from Staffordshire and Buckinghamshire brick around a concrete frame. A single concrete pillar supports the ticket hall ceiling, still with its original ticket 'passimeter' at the base and an interior featuring bronze and wooden fixtures and fittings. The bridge leading down to the platforms is of unpolished (but now painted) concrete. Holden's assistant Charles Hutton worked closely on this station, rearranging some of the details of Holden's initial design to accommodate the radical exposed concrete frame.

Station building: 1932

Designed by: Charles Holden

Listed: Grade II*

ARNOS GROVE
UNDERGROUND
Except local buses
ARNOS GROVE

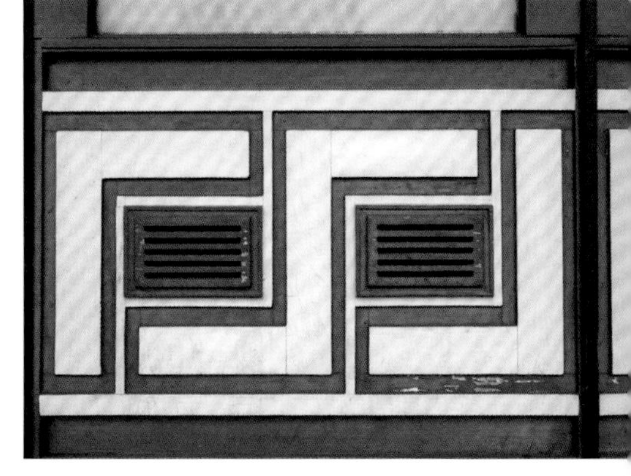

SOUTHGATE

Here Holden produces a purely circular station building, without the square base seen at Arnos Grove and other stations. The roof appears to undulate like a tent canvas, thanks to the thin concrete design produced by assistant Israel Schultz. Inside, as at Arnos Grove, a single concrete pole supports the roof with a passimeter at the base. The curving theme is repeated in the bus and shopping parade, which coils around the station, allowing buses to sweep in from the road. The exterior also features masts that were designed to combine lighting, seating and timetables.

Station building: 1933

Designed by: Charles Holden

Listed: Grade II*

SOUTHGATE STATION
ROUTE 66
SUITS
£99
SALE

OAKWOOD

From the outside, Oakwood appears to be just another brick-box style station, but this functional appearance belies many interesting design points. The plan is similar to stations like Acton Town and Sudbury Town, but with extra windows to allow more daylight and an extended canopy at the front. The ticket hall is spacious, with shops and facilities as part of the civic hub ideal. The platforms feature cantilevered concrete canopies designed by Stanley Heaps. It was often Heaps's task to develop the more mundane details, but here and at other stations like Chiswick Park and Ealing Common, his platform shelters rise to the occasion, balancing poise and purpose.

Station building: 1932

Designed by: Charles Holden

Listed: Grade II*

OAKWOOD STATION

COCKFOSTERS

The terminus of the extension is the most atypical, and perhaps, most interesting of Holden's station designs. Two straightforward surface buildings lead down to a long, nave-like space containing the ticket hall and platform areas, partly covered by the train shed. The structure is of reinforced, board-marked concrete, lit from above by large clerestory windows achieving a grandeur not often seen at such a minor stop. The intended plan for the station was to have two towers on either side of the road where the current buildings are. Ultimately, the current design was used with an eye on building shops and even a cinema on top as the suburbs grew. Due to the Green Belt Act after the World War II, the spread of semis was checked, and the station was left alone.

Station building: 1933

Designed by: Charles Holden

Listed: Grade II

UNDERGROUND
COCKFOSTERS STATION
UNDERGROUND
New laughs have landed
7888

UNDERGROUND
Danger

REPEAT PERFORMANCE : THE DISTRICT LINE EAST 1932–1935

The District Line originated as the District Railway, one of the first underground railway companies to operate in London. The District had a history of collaboration (and falling out) with the Metropolitan Railway, another company that gave its name to a tube line. Together, they operated the Inner Circle, the forerunner of today's Circle Line, in addition to individual spur lines. The District ran services to Hounslow, Richmond, Ealing and Whitechapel, and jointly with the Met to Uxbridge. Their ambitions, which often seemed to run ahead of their finances, even stretched to briefly running services to Windsor and Southend. The company was eventually purchased by Charles Yerkes and his Underground Electric Railways of London company in 1901 via an investment vehicle that paid for the electrification of the District's lines. This integration with the UERL meant Frank Pick oversaw the District, and when he overhauled the tube network's image in the 1920s and 1930s, many stations on the line were redesigned by Charles Holden. Stations at Sudbury Town, Acton Town and Chiswick Park, initially built in the contemporary turn-of-the-century fashion of dark brick, slate roofs and small ticket halls, were replaced by European-influenced buildings combining concrete, brick, steel and glass.

As well as the Met, the District Railway had also forged a relationship with the London, Midland & Scottish Railway (LMS), who took over the running of several services. With the line beyond East Ham unelectrified, District Railway services to Upminster had been suspended in 1905 when the company's trains were converted to electric traction. However, a new commuter base developed in the area during the 1920s thanks to the London County Council estate at Becontree. Home to 100,000 people, the LMS saw an opportunity to increase capacity with the addition of seven new stations, upgrading and electrifying the line at the same time. Electric trains began running on 4 September 1932, with passenger services commencing the following week.

The LMS were responsible for designing and building the stations through their chief architect William Henry Hamlyn. Hamlyn was born in Wigan in 1889, studying at the Liverpool School of Architecture before working for the London & North Western Railway. He later joined the LMS and designed train stations, hotels, offices and training centres. His designs for the Upminster branch were functional brick buildings often built over the railway line, with Upminster Bridge being the most visually interesting of the set.

UPNEY / BECONTREE / DAGENHAM HEATHWAY / HORNCHURCH

Most of the Upminster extension stations follow a pattern; a single-storey ticket hall in red brick, situated on a bridge over the railway line, with an 'UNDERGROUND' roundel on a pole. A parapet with vertical brickwork brings a small amount of interest to the exterior. The interior of the small ticket hall is finished in cream and green tile work and is passed through quickly. Passengers are transported down the platform area by a long wooden walkway, where they will find brick waiting rooms and canopies supported by iron columns painted green. Many of the stations still have the old wooden LMS benches on the platforms. This kit plan prefigured Hamlyn's post-war work in designing prefabricated station designs to be used on bomb-damaged sites. At the end of the platform at Upney, beyond the passenger area, are a couple of early prefabricated concrete bridge walkways used to take train crew to the depot area.

Station buildings: 1932

Designed by: William H Hamlyn

BECONTREE STATION

DAGENHAM HEATHWAY STATION
District line

HORNCHURCH STATION
HORNCHURCH KIOSK

DAGENHAM EAST

Dagenham East is much like the previously mentioned stations between Upney and Hornchurch but survives in better condition. It has a single-storey brick ticket hall which sits on a bridge viaduct over the railway line. The roofline has a stepped profile, with a roundel and pole sign above the central entrance. All of these 'identikit' stations originally featured windows in the facade, as can still be seen at Hornchurch, but at Dagenham East, they are in-filled and used to house information display frames. The station opened in 1885 as Dagenham, as part of London, Tilbury & Southend Railway. It was rebuilt by the LMS in 1932 for the electrification of the line, and the 'East' was added in May 1949. The station was refurbished in 2006, with 21st-century station essentials such as CCTV and help points added. The platforms have brick waiting rooms and canopies supported by iron columns.

Station building: 1932

Designed by: William H Hamlyn

DAGENHAM EAST
DAGENHAM EAST STATION

ELM PARK

Elm Park was the last of the Upminster branch stations to be completed, opening on 13 May 1935, nearly two years after the District Railway had ceased to be. Designed and run like the other stations by the LMS, Elm Park had some subtle design differences from its preceding stations. Similarly, the ticket office is positioned on a viaduct over the tracks and is a one-storey building of brick. In this instance, the ends of the roof are given a streamlined curve, a subtle nod to the Art Deco stylings used at other transport hubs of the era. Around this and above the entrance was the station name and LMS in stylised metal letting. Sadly these have long been removed, and the curved profile is somewhat denuded by metal safety railing. A sloping wooden walkway connects the ticket hall to the platform, which features metal canopy shelters.

Station building: 1935

Designed by: William H Hamlyn

UNDERGROUND
ELM PARK STATION
ELM PARK MINI CABS
Your Local Car Service
01708 47 77 77
01708 44 20 20
AIRPORT TRANSFERS
LOCAL & LONG DISTANCE
ALL STATION TRANSFERS
ALL PORTS TRANSFERS
SCHOOL RUNS
ANY TIME, ANYWHERE

UPMINSTER BRIDGE

The most individual of the Upminster extension stations, Upminster Bridge, opened on 17 December 1934. Like the others, the construction is of dark brown brick, but here in a more interesting arrangement, with vertical and horizontal bonding giving greater visual interest than the previous stations. There is a double-height ticket hall with a polygonal brick second floor featuring a glass-brick roof light. The most eye-catching part of the interior is the swastika design inlaid in the terrazzo floor. This ancient religious icon was used widely in the Western world at the start of the century before its co-optation by the Nazi party. The ticket hall also features a restored K4 red telephone box. A walkway takes passengers up to the platform area. Here you can find a couple of distinctive curved red wooden benches. They originally sported enamel station names signs, now removed.

Station building: 1934

Designed by: William H Hamlyn

UNDERGROUND
PLUMBING SUPPLIES
K. WAGSTAFF & SONS
PLUMBING & HEATING SUPPLIERS
01708 - 437211 / 473043
UPMINSTER BRIDGE
Little India
K. WAGSTAFF & SONS
CENTRAL HEATING & PLUMBING
FLASH
BUS

Way out
Informati

FIVE-YEAR PLAN : THE NEW WORKS PROGRAMME 1935–1939

Fresh from the success of the Piccadilly Line extensions and having amalgamated the many disparate companies into the London Transport Passenger Board, Frank Pick sought to continue the modernisation of the network with the New Works Programme. This five-year plan incorporated the rebuilding of many older stations, in addition to further expansion out into the suburbs. However, as so often happens, the moment of greatest triumph was also the beginning of the end. This was where the upward curve of creative brilliance that began with the Northern Line extension of 1926 crested and started to take a downward turn.

Charles Holden had taken on the redesign of the University of London in Bloomsbury. The project, which was initially to stretch 1,200 feet along the street, was slimmed down due to lack of funds, with Senate House being the only completed part. In his absence, Holden was replaced by a number of other architects, all producing imitations of his work. A similar approach had worked on the eastbound Piccadilly Line extension but was less successful here. Holden had to help redesign some of the stations, such as Rayners Lane and East Finchley, in a bid to maintain the high standards set in previous years. Even the stations directly designed by Holden, like Eastcote, do not show the great leaps forward seen between the mid-1920s and early 1930s.

Several of the stations were given entirely to Stanley Heaps. Those he produced, St. John's Wood, Harrow-on-the-Hill and a new entrance for Earl's Court, are well designed, but stick to the Holden template without adding much new. As well as the rebuilt stations, the New Works Programme planned for two new line extensions. One was three stations on the eastbound Central Line (see p145), the other was the Northern Heights project, which aimed to extend the Northern Line into Hertfordshire. Two stations would have been rebuilt (Highgate and Finchley Central) and three new stations constructed (Brockley Hill, Elstree South and Bushey Heath). World War II and the Green Belt Act of 1938, put paid to these ambitions, with little money or political will to extend the line northwards thereafter.

PARK ROYAL

Built to replace the original District Railway station from 1903, Park Royal is an excellent example of Frank Pick's drive to introduce a more eye-catching look to the tube network. The new station, designed by Herbert Welch and Felix Lander, was needed to serve the neighbouring Hanger Hill estate – also the work of Welch and Lander. The building, situated next to Western Avenue, makes its presence felt with a tall, square tower sporting the Underground roundel on each side. The ticket hall is a circular design, which along with the tower and the curved parade of shops, makes up a visually engaging arrangement of volumes from different angles.

Station building: 1936

Designed by: Herbert Welch and Felix Lander

Listed: Grade II

UNDERGROUND
UNDERGROUND
24HR MINICABS
PARK ROYAL STATION
24/7

SOUTH HARROW

The Piccadilly Line had replaced the District Railway here in 1932, but South Harrow had to wait three more years for a new station, opening on 5 July 1935. The Holden-designed station straddles the tracks, with the entrance to a small ticket hall area underneath the platforms. Seen from the street, the station steps up towards the railway viaduct, with a ground-floor shop on one side. The station also features a small integrated bus station, part of Pick's civic hub concept, seeking to integrate transport networks.

Station building: 1935

Designed by: Charles Holden

UNDERGROUND
BAG REPAIRS
SHOE REPAIRS
LEATHER JACKETS REPAIRED
SHOE REPAIRS
TOPY
SOUTH HARROW STATION

RAYNERS LANE

By 1938, a house-building boom and resulting population increase necessitated a new station at Rayners Lane. The area was speculatively called 'Harrow Garden Village', but the station was named after the lane that led to Rayners Farm. The old country halt was replaced with a Holden-style box courtesy of New Zealand-born architect Reginald Uren, famous for his design of Hornsey Town Hall and previously an assistant to Holden. The new ticket hall sits over the tracks, with curved flanks that contain kiosks. The platform spaces feature waiting rooms, exposed brick walls and concrete columns half-covered with brown tiling.

Station building: 1938

Designed by: Reginald Uren and Charles Holden

Listed: Grade II

RAYNERS LANE STATION

EASTCOTE

A number of potential designs were produced in the process of finding a new station for Eastcote, including one with a rounded front, and intriguingly, an all-glass ticket hall. In the end, the station is somewhat of a retread of previous ideas. The design is similar to Rayners Lane, with the box ticket hall flanked by two rounded kiosks, both topped with eye-catching roundels on masts. Holden had stepped away from designing stations for the New Works Programme due to his University of London commission but was persuaded to return by Pick when the new designs fell from the previous high standards.

Station building: 1939

Designed by: Charles Holden

Listed: Grade II

LUNCH · SANDWICHES · BURGERS
STCOTE CAFE
ACC 0208 868
UNDERGROUND
EASTCOTE STATION
Minicabs
UNDERGROUND
EASTCOTE NEWS BOX LTD

RUISLIP MANOR

Like South Harrow, Ruislip Manor abuts the railway with entrances on both sides of the bridge. Alternative design solutions were considered, including a scheme using prefabricated parts that could be replicated at other sites on the line. In the end, simplicity and economy won out, with the twin entrances part of a small parade of shops and the staircases tower and platform areas above them. The most interesting part of the interior is the number-free Art Deco-style clock at the bottom of the stairs. The platforms have concrete shelters, but these lack the assurance of Stanley Heaps's earlier shelter designs at stations like Oakwood and Chiswick Park. Further down the platform is an original wooden shelter from 1912 when the station was named Ruislip Manor Halt.

Station building: 1938

Designed by: Charles Holden

UNDERGROUND
RUISLIP MANOR STATION
RVP
SAP
HALIFAX
WE'RE LOOKING OUT FOR YOU

UXBRIDGE

The terminus station of the Metropolitan and Piccadilly Lines has an incongruously grand facade, the result of the collaboration between Charles Holden, Leonard Bucknell and Ruth Ellis. The new station replaced a 1904 Metropolitan Railway station located on the outskirts of the town. Bucknell and Ellis's original design proved too large and expensive for the budget, so Holden revised the scheme adding a Cockfosters-style train shed. The front facade, decorated with sculptures by Joseph Armitage, curves around a now pedestrianised area, complete with an illuminated roundel sign. Inside, the ticket hall is lit by clerestory windows and stained glass work by Ervin Bossányi, continuing into the reinforced concrete structure covering the platform areas.

Station building: 1938

Designed by: LH Bucknell, Ruth Ellis and Charles Holden

Listed: Grade II

METROPOLITAN & PICCADILLY LINES
UXBRIDGE
TUI
Sweet Express
CONFECTIONERY · TOBACCO · PHONE CARDS · OYSTER · NEWS
Oyster Ticket Stop

EAST FINCHLEY

Like Uxbridge, East Finchley station results from an original design by Bucknell and Ellis with some revisions by Charles Holden. This building replaced the 1867 Great Northern Railway station and was the terminus of the Northern Line until 1940. The new station is built around the four-track viaduct that goes underground slightly to the south. Viewed from the street, the building doesn't have the same visual clarity as earlier Holden-era buildings but makes up for this at platform level. Here, the open platforms have streamlined waiting rooms and a statue of an archer by Eric Aumonier. Over the tracks sits a building containing offices and staff rooms with prominent glazed towers incorporating spiral staircases. The station is the only building completed as part of the ill-fated Northern Heights project.

Station building: 1939–42

Designed by: LH Bucknell, Ruth Ellis and Charles Holden

Listed: Grade II

EAST FINCHLEY STATION
Tea
Cafe

EARL'S COURT

Earl's Court is a mixture of many eras. The station opened in 1871, with the current Earl's Court Road entrance by Harry W Ford dating from 1906. The spacious train shed dates from 1878 by John Wolfe Barry, the engineer for Tower Bridge. An additional entrance was added on Warwick Road in 1937 to serve the newly built exhibition centre (demolished in 2014). This was designed by Stanley Heaps using the circular motif as seen at Southgate and later St. John's Wood. The structure is in brown brick, with an interior of blue and cream tiles. In 1970 a glass rotunda, which acts as a control room, was added on top. The platforms feature wooden benches with roundel backrests and period train-indicator boards.

Station buildings: 1937

Designed by: Stanley Heaps

Listed: Grade II

UNDERGROUND
EARL'S COURT STATION
One way

ALDGATE EAST

Opened in 1884 as part of the District Railway, Aldgate East was rebuilt in 1938 with the train tracks realigned, and the platforms moved. The new platforms were given a clean, modern appearance, much lighter and more spacious than the previous Victorian era ones. The platforms feature Harold Stabler's relief tiles, as seen at St. John's Wood and Bethnal Green. New entrances were added, which were finished in cream tile with blue trim.

The station was redeveloped in 2007 removing the 1938 entrances but leaving the District and Hammersmith & City line platforms intact.

Station buildings: 1938

Designed by: Stanley Heaps

£30

HARROW ON THE HILL

Built at the foot of Harrow Hill to replace the 1880 Metropolitan Railway building, these days it is hard to get a good view of the Heaps-designed station as later structures have almost entirely surrounded it. The original design had a much grander station than was built, with a curved forecourt. The station as-built straddles the tracks, providing access from both north and south. The south entrance has a large window with coloured roundel and original circular lamps. The centre of the station is a tower rising over the tracks containing an electric signal cabin, accessed by a spiral staircase. The platforms feature the island waiting rooms topped with gull-wing roofs and combination concrete name slabs and lamps.

Station building: 1939–43

Designed by: Stanley Heaps

UNDERGROUND
HARROW ON THE
ILL STATION
2 Metres
Please stay 2m apart for everyone's safety.

A BOROUGH
BRENT
BOROUGH
STANDARD

BEFORE THE JUBILEE :
THE BAKERLOO LINE NORTH
1936–1939

The Bakerloo Line started life as the Baker Street and Waterloo Railway, opened in 1906 by the Underground Electric Railways Company of London (UERL). It ran between Baker Street and Lambeth North, extending first south to Elephant & Castle, then west through Queen's Park and on to Watford.

As part of the New Works Programme, carried out between 1935 and 1940, the Bakerloo Line was extended northwest from Baker Street to Stanmore to help relieve congestion on the Metropolitan Line. The work primarily consisted of new platforms and passenger facilities, with brand new stations at St. John's Wood, Swiss Cottage and Queensbury.

The design work was carried out by London Transport's in-house architect department, led by Stanley Heaps, who adopted the Moderne style brought to the network by Charles Holden. The most recognisable design element of the reconstructions is the swooping concrete canopies and curved glass shelters installed on the platforms of Kilburn and Dollis Hill. They are a simple but powerful use of the streamlined aesthetic favoured throughout the 1930s to denote speed and style. The palette used for the new interior areas tended to be predominantly cream tiling with colour trim, an arrangement seen at other New Works Programme-era stations like Bethnal Green, Aldgate East and Highgate.

This Stanmore branch of the Bakerloo Line opened on 20 November 1939. Forty years later, it was transferred to the Jubilee Line, moving over to the newly opened service on 1 May 1979.

Shelter on Kilburn station platform

ST. JOHN'S WOOD

A new station in leafy St. John's Wood was built as part of the Bakerloo extension, replacing the nearby Lord's/St. John's Wood station from 1925. Stanley Heaps produced a circular design for the street-level ticket hall, reminiscent of Warren Street or Southgate. As at Warren Street, the ticket hall was later built over, with flats added in 1960. There is a planted area in front of the entrance that includes an unexpected pair of palm trees. Inside, the ticket hall is a mixture of pale tilework and exposed brick. The escalators feature 58 bronze uplighters leading down to the platform concourse. The platforms themselves feature a full set of Harold Stabler's relief tiles, depicting various London landmarks such as the Houses of Parliament, St. Paul's Cathedral and Thomas Lord, who the nearby cricket ground is named after.

Station building: 1939

Designed by: Stanley Heaps

Listed: Grade II

ST. JOHN'S WOOD STATION
ST. JOHN'S WOOD STATION

SWISS COTTAGE

A station named Swiss Cottage had been opened by the Metropolitan Railway in 1868, rebuilt in the 1920s by CW Clark, and then closed in 1940. A new station was opened in 1939 adjacent to the old with no street-level buildings, although a lollypop roundel and ventilation tower denoted the entrance. The subterranean ticket hall is finished with cream tiling on the walls and a green speckled design on the floor. The escalators to the platform are typical of the New Works Programme stations, with a staircase down the middle and bronze uplighters along the way. The top and bottom of the escalators also feature 'WAY OUT' and 'TO TRAINS' backlit roundels. The platforms are finished in the same cream tile as the ticket hall, with green and brown trim with the station name in black lettering. The original ventilation tower was replaced in 1979 with the current black brick totem.

Station building: 1939

Designed by: Stanley Heaps

ONE APP.
ALL YOUR
FAVOURITES.

WAY OUT

SWISS COTTAGE

FINCHLEY ROAD

Finchley Road station opened as part of the Metropolitan Railways extension from Swiss Cottage to West Hampstead in 1879. It was rebuilt in 1911 by Frank Sherrin, son of George, with extra tracks, an island platform and a new ticket hall. The station was reconstructed again in 1939 for the Bakerloo Line takeover. Sherrin's two-storey design was modified, with a Portland stone facade replacing the previous stone finish. The interior of the ticket hall was finished in the cream tiling and grey St. James floor tiles used elsewhere on this line. Another island platform was added to cope with the new traffic, and the passenger areas were covered with a partly glazed canopy.

Station building: 1939

Designed by: Stanley Heaps

CANFIELD
GARDENS
FINCHLEY ROAD STATION
UNDERGROUND
free cash
withdrawals
free cash
withdrawals
RVP
Keep out
BOOK A
COVID TEST

KILBURN

Kilburn station was originally opened by the Metropolitan Railway in 1879 as Kilburn & Brondesbury. This part of its heritage can still be seen with the Met's name spelt out along the bridge that carries the tracks over Kilburn High Road. The station entrance was reconstructed in 1915 to allow widening of the track. In 1939 the building was given new finishes when transferred to the Bakerloo Line, including glass bricks and the same cream and grey colour scheme as neighbouring stations. The most striking part of the 1930s redesign is the streamlined platform canopies, with their curving gull-wing roofline. The station name was shortened purely to Kilburn in 1950 and it became part of the Jubilee line in 1979.

Station building: 1939

Designed by: Stanley Heaps

KILBURN STATION
KILBURN STATION
KILBURN FLOWERS

DOLLIS HILL

Dollis Hill has two very modest entrances, with passageways leading through to a small ticket hall, then up to the platform area. It was opened in 1909 by the Met, after pressure from local property developers eager to have a transport connection next to their new estates. Internally, the station features the same finishes as the other Bakerloo stations, including a distinctive platform canopy with a curving, overhanging roof sitting above a waiting room in red brick. The entrance passages are enlivened with enamel panels by artist Amanda Duncan. Designed in 1995, they depict maps of the local area throughout the ages.

Station building: 1939

Designed by: Stanley Heaps

DOLLIS HILL STATION
UNDERGROUND

QUEENSBURY

Queensbury is quite different in form from most of the London Transport stations of the 1930s, more in keeping with the suburban Metropolitan Railway stations of CW Clark, like neighbouring Kingsbury. As at that station, Queensbury is built as part of a parade of shops and flats. The building is a typically 1930s three-storey parade in brick, with shops fronting the street and flats above. The most distinctive part of the station is opposite the entrance, a tall 'mushroom' shelter with a large roundel and pole sign. The idea is very similar to those shelters found on the Piccadilly Line, outside Southgate and Oakwood, but its curving concrete form is more forward-looking than those designs. Another point of interest is the 'UNDERGROUND' name bars which protrude into the street, letting uncertain passengers know where the entrance is.

Station building: 1936

Designed by: Stanley Heaps

Bake & Bite
Cakes | Hot & cold drinks
Lebara
UNDERGROUND
QUEENSBURY STATION
UNDERGROUND
Lebara
mobile
020 87283000

Way out
NEWBURY PARK

BRANCHING OUT : THE CENTRAL LINE EAST 1940–1948

What we know today as the Central Line began in July 1900 as the Central London Railway with six stations from Liverpool Street to Shepherd's Bush. This is how the line stayed until the mid-1930s when the newly created London Transport Passenger Board under Frank Pick sought to extend the line eastwards and westwards as had been done with the Piccadilly Line a few years before. The eastwards extension of the Central Line would expand the service from Liverpool Street out into Essex.

This area was the territory of the London & North Eastern Railway, which ran a suburban branch to Epping and Ongar from Liverpool Street. The Central Line replaced and expanded this service with additional stations in the growing eastern suburbs. New tunnels were built to connect the stations with the existing LNER stops and link with the District Line. Construction on the new stations and tunnels had begun as part of the 1935–40 New Works Programme but was put on hold when World War II broke out. The half-built stations were often used as air-raid shelters or as underground factories. Building resumed after the war, but shortages of materials and manpower led to redesigns of the station buildings and plans for expansion.

Before war broke out, the LNER had begun building one station in anticipation of the Central Line takeover. Loughton opened in 1940 and was designed by John Murray Easton in a recognisably London Transport style. Oliver Hill was the LNER's design consultant and was given the job of overseeing the redesign of the stations from Stratford onwards. The only project completed by Hill was a new bus shelter for Newbury Park station. The rest of his plan was cancelled after the war due to a lack of funds.

Charles Holden was commissioned to design three stations for the extension; Wanstead, Redbridge and Gants Hill. These would prove to be the last he would produce for London Transport. Once again, the three buildings' final form differed somewhat from the original designs due to post-war privations. Wanstead and Redbridge were shorn of the glass walls that would have possibly signalled a new direction from Holden, and Gants Hill lost its clock tower.

Signal box at Newbury Park station

LIVERPOOL STREET

Liverpool Street Railway Station first opened in 1875 as the Great Eastern Railway terminus from Norwich and King's Lynn. The same year it was connected to the underground Metropolitan Railway, initially named Bishopsgate. It became part of the Central London Railway (later Central Line) in 1912 and was later used as an air-raid shelter during World War II. In 1946 the Central Line was extended eastwards with Liverpool Street receiving new entrances and a ticket hall. The entrance on Old Broad Street and Liverpool Street has the hallmarks of the 1946 extension, a windowless facade in cream tile with roundels projecting into the street.

Station building: 1946–51

Designed by: Stanley Heaps and Thomas Bilbow

UNDERGROUND
UNDERGROUND
LIVERPOOL STREET UNDERGROUND STATION

BETHNAL GREEN

Construction on Bethnal Green started before World War II, with the station eventually opening to Central Line services on 4 December 1946. Like many others, the station had been used as an air-raid shelter during the war. Tragically on 3 March 1943, 173 people were killed in a crush when an entrance became blocked during a raid. The station has no notable above-ground buildings apart from a combined kiosk, shelter and ventilation shaft in Bethnal Green Gardens. The ticket hall and platform areas are finished in pale yellow tiling manufactured by Poole Pottery. The platforms feature Harold Stabler's relief tiles, with symbols and buildings of London, as seen at St. John's Wood.

Station building: 1946

Designed by: Charles Holden and Stanley Heaps

UNDERGROUND
BETHNAL GREEN
PUBLIC SUBWAY
COFFEE | BREAKFAST | LUNCH | DINNER | COCKTAILS
TOWER HAMLETS

MILE END

Mile End was first opened in June 1902 as part of the Whitechapel & Bow Railway, later serving the District and Metropolitan Lines. A rebuild of the station integrated the new Central Line services from Liverpool Street, opening on 4 December 1946. A new street entrance was built, with a subterranean ticket hall. The above-ground building is reminiscent of Holden's early screen designs, with a rectangular face clad in cream tile. The station is one of the relatively few London Underground stations to have a cross-platform interchange, with two island platforms in cream and green tile, giving it the air of the New York Subway.

Station building: 1946

Designed by: Stanley Heaps and Thomas Bilbow

MILE END
LONDON TRANSPORT
UNDERGROUND
MILE END STATION
Paddy Power
CLEANERS

LEYTONSTONE

Leytonstone was another station rebuilt to accommodate the new Central Line extension eastwards. Its history shares the same trajectory as its neighbour, Leyton. It opened in 1856 for the Eastern Counties Railway, before becoming part of the Great Eastern Railway in 1867, then the LNER in 1923. Unlike Leyton, a totally new station building and platforms were constructed for the Central Line takeover. Construction had started before World War II but was halted in May 1940. The new station building, opened in May 1947, is a single-storey brick structure with a curved entrance leading into a long passenger tunnel to the above-ground platforms. The entrance and tunnel now feature mosaics celebrating the work of local hero Alfred Hitchcock created by the Greenwich Mural Workshop in 1999–2001 to commemorate the centenary of his birth.

Station building: 1947

Designed by: Thomas Bilbow

UNDERGROUND
PUBLIC SUBWAY
LEYTONSTONE STATION
STATION SHOEREPAIRS & KEYS
KEYS CUT
WHILE-U-WAIT
SHOE REPAIRS
ENGRAVING

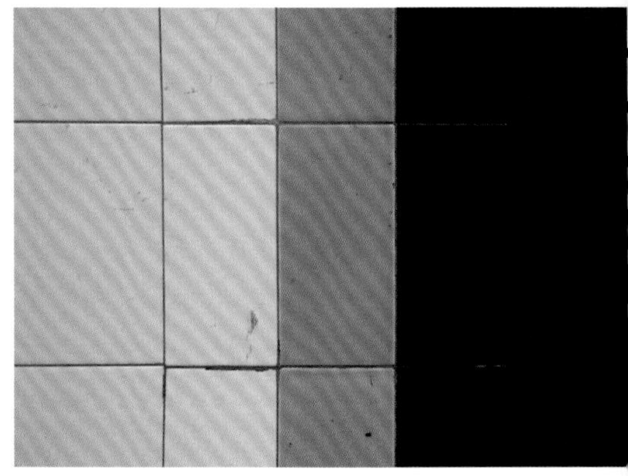

WANSTEAD

Wanstead went through many variations in design, including a cross-shaped ticket hall with a bus interchange similar to Southgate. Ultimately, a rectangular plan was chosen, balanced by a ventilation tower in glass brick and featuring a carving of St. George and the Dragon by Joseph Armitage. However, after the war the design was revised, with the glass brick and carving making way for prefabricated concrete panels finished in grey render and black tile around the entrance. Inside, the ticket hall is spacious and plain, with glass bricks bringing in light. Wanstead, Redbridge and Gants Hill stations were used as air-raid shelters during the war, while Plessey Electronics occupied the unused tunnels in between for manufacturing munitions.

Station building: 1940–7

Designed by: Charles Holden

UNDER GROUND
UNDERGROUND
UNDERGROUND
WANSTEAD STATION
WANSTEAD STATION

REDBRIDGE

Like Wanstead, the original design for Redbridge would have utilised large quantities of glass in a way not previously seen in Holden's stations. The ticket hall was to be almost totally translucent, with a glass ventilation tower incorporating an etching from the 1937 Paris Exposition. The tower and rounded plan were kept for the final building, but the glass was replaced with cheaper brick and tile. The exterior features railings with design motifs of roundels and 'LT' symbols, as well as a totem signpost. The ticket hall has a circular ceiling design, with 12 concrete spokes radiating out from the centre. The platforms are finished with Poole Pottery tiling in cream, blue and black, and feature two original platform clocks with roundels in place of the numbers.

Station building: 1939–47

Designed by: Charles Holden

Listed: Grade II

UNDERGROUND
UNDERGROUND
REDBRIDGE STATION

GANTS HILL

Gants Hill has virtually no above-ground buildings, with a planned clock tower being dropped, but its beauty lies underground. Subway pedestrian tunnels lead down to a subterranean ticket hall lit by square Art Deco roof lights. Down the escalators is the Moscow Metro-inspired concourse area, probably the best of Holden's time with the Underground. The concourse is 150 ft long with a domed ceiling and finished in cream tiles with orange trim. The idea for a Moscow-style station was pushed by Frank Pick, with London Transport having close links with the Soviet authorities since their visit to see the Piccadilly Circus rebuild and a subsequent visit by London Transport officials to Moscow in 1935. With Gants Hill, the circle of influence was complete.

Station building: 1937–47

Designed by: Charles Holden

Listed: Grade II

NEWBURY PARK

The rebuilding of Newbury Park, which opened in 1903, was planned to accommodate the increase in expected passenger numbers when joining the Central Line and facilitate the widening of Eastern Avenue. Oliver Hill, who was consultant architect to the LNER, was tasked to design the new tube station and bus interchange. Hill and his assistant Edward Duley prepared a scheme in 1937 that included a streamlined ticket hall in brick, sitting alongside the concrete bus shelter. After the interruption of war, the bus shelter was completed, but the station plans were dropped and alterations made to the existing facilities. The shelter is constructed of reinforced concrete with Chesil Beach aggregate, and the roof is covered in copper sheets. Like White City, Newbury Park won a Festival of Britain 'Award for Merit' in 1951.

Station building: 1948

Designed by: Oliver Hill

Listed: Grade II*

GRANGE HILL

Originally opened as a stop on the Fairlop Loop line in 1903, plans for a new station at Grange Hill were drawn up in advance of the impending Central Line takeover. Construction began in 1938, but was suspended on the outbreak of war, with the original station building later damaged by a V-2 rocket in 1944. Work was recommenced after the war, with the new station finally opening in November 1948. The ticket hall is a brick box with a strip of windows on either side of the building. The compact interior space is finished in exposed brick and cream tiling with stairs leading down to the platform areas, which have the 1903 canopies intact.

Station building: 1948

Designed by: Thomas Bilbow

UNDERGROUND
UNDERGROUND
GRANGE HILL STATION
EMERGENCY VEHICLES
ONLY

LEYTON / SOUTH WOODFORD / RODING VALLEY / HAINAULT

These four stations were all part of the Central Line extension of 1946–8, and benefited from improvements to varying degrees.

Leyton, which opened in 1856 as part of the Eastern Counties Railway, had a new facade in cream tile added with projecting roundel signs to catch the eyes of the potential customers. The small ticket hall was redone in cream tile, with automatic ticket machines included as well.

South Woodford had a new brick entrance added on the eastern side of the station in 1947. It had initially been called 'George Lane' before becoming 'South Woodford (George Lane)' in 1937 for a short period. Signs with that name can still be seen on the platforms.

Roding Valley also had a single-storey brick entrance added to its temporary 1936 station, opening in 1949.

Hainault has a similarly subdued entrance wedged under the railway bridge. However, the platform area is more interesting with gull-wing style waiting rooms and concrete name signs. You can also glimpse the Hainault Train Depot from 1939, complete with an Art Deco clock.

Station buildings: 1946–9

Designed by: Thomas Bilbow

LEYTON STATION

SOUTH WOODFORD STATION

UNDERGROUND
RODING VALLEY STATION

LOUGHTON

The current Loughton station is the third station to serve the town, opening in 1940 and joining the Central Line in 1948. The new station was designed by John Easton Murray of Stanley Hall, Easton & Robertson, his only station. The redevelopment was overseen by the LNER and London Transport, bearing the hallmarks of both companies' history. The ticket hall, built in golden brown brick around a reinforced concrete frame, is influenced by both Holden stations of the 1930s and the LNER terminal at King's Cross, as seen in the half-moon main window. The front of the station features a bus interchange and a small parade of shops, keeping the civic hub idea alive. The platforms have two wonderful curving passenger shelters in concrete with porthole roof lights.

Station building: 1940

Designed by: John Easton Murray

Listed: Grade II

LOUGHTON STATION
Raysam's
No parking
DRIVERS REQUIRED
APPLY WITHIN or call
020 8508 6600
SADLERS TAXIS
BOOK & TRACK
DOWNLOAD SADLERS NEW AP.

THE LONG GOODBYE : THE CENTRAL LINE WEST 1940–1961

As the extension of the Central Line to the east replaced the service of London & North Eastern Railway, the westwards extension would replace the service provided by the Great Western Railway's New North Main Line. To compensate the GWR for this loss of business, the commission for the new stations was given to their in-house architects' department. As a result, in this chapter, we are not looking at the work of Charles Holden or Stanley Heaps but mainly that of Brian Lewis and later, Frederick Curtis.

Brian Lewis was born in Tasmania in 1906, studying architecture at first in Melbourne and then after moving to Britain, in Liverpool. After graduating, he moved to London and went to work for the Great Western Railway architects department under Percy Culverhouse. Lewis was given the task of designing five new stations, one at West Acton, then four more for the extension to West Ruislip. West Acton, however, would be the only station Lewis would see completed. The opening of the others was delayed by World War II, with the designs revised by Frederick Curtis. Lewis left the GWR and Britain in 1947 to head the architecture department of Melbourne University.

Curtis was born in Frankfurt, Germany, in 1903. His father was a prominent Jewish lecturer in English at the University of Darmstadt, and when the Nazis came to power, the family fled to Britain. The Curtis family would subsequently be placed in the SS 'Black Book', a document listing British residents to be arrested after a successful invasion. After lecturing at the Liverpool School of Architecture, Curtis worked for the Southern Railway, then as an assistant to Charles Holden before moving to the GWR. He took over from Lewis and then became the Chief Architect of British Rail in 1948 when the railway system was nationalised. The building of the new stations for the western extension of the Central Line was postponed on the outbreak of war, and when peace came, the original designs were revised to account for post-war shortages of materials. The stations opened for service in 1947, but many of the buildings would not be complete until the early 1960s.

Platform at West Acton station

WHITE CITY

White City station was built to replace the old Wood Lane station, which opened in 1908 as the western terminus for the Central London Railway. The new building was constructed just to the north of the old station, opening on 23 November 1947. It was designed by architects AD McGill and Kenneth Seymour, under the supervision of Thomas Bilbow, who had succeeded Stanley Heaps as Chief Architect of London Transport. They produced a Holdenesque design, with a cuboid ticket hall, featuring large glass windows with a coloured roundel. The platform areas feature wooden combination station signs and seats, similar to those found on the Piccadilly Line Cockfosters extension. The station won a Festival of Britain design award in 1951, and the Abram Games-designed plaque can be seen to the left of the entrance.

Station building: 1947

Designed by: Seymour, Bilbow and McGill

CAFE
FRESH JUICE
SMOOTHIES
PORRIGE
UNDERGROUND
UNDERGROUND
UNDERGROUND
WHITE CITY STATION

WEST ACTON

West Acton is an interesting example of the next step from the Holden-style brick box. The above-ground building replaced the original station of 1923 and consists of a ticket hall with full-height glazing at the front and rear, sandwiched by two brick side walls built around a concrete frame. Leading down to the platforms is a tiled covered concrete footbridge with bronze railings. On each platform is a waiting area, complete with beautifully curved hardwood benches. West Acton was the only station finished to Lewis's original designs. By the time his other Central Line designs had been completed after the war, Lewis had returned to Australia.

Station building: 1940

Designed by: Brian Lewis

Listed: Grade II

WEST ACTON
STATION
WEST
ACTON
STATION
UNDERGROUND

HANGER LANE

Like the other new stations heading west on the Central Line, construction at Hanger Lane began before World War II but was not completed until 1949, with a temporary station employed from 1947. Brian Lewis's design is a relative of Charles Holden's circular stations like Southgate, formed of a drum ticket hall with a concrete canopy over the entrance. The interior of the ticket hall is below street level, lit by the clerestory windows, with a single bronze uplighter in the centre of the hall. Lewis's original design was revised by FCC Curtis and Peter MacIver to account for the post-war lack of materials and advancement in building techniques.

Station building: 1947

Designed by: Brian Lewis, FCC Curtis and Peter MacIver

HANGER
STATION

PERIVALE

Like the next stop along Greenford, Perivale nestles against the railway viaduct, with passengers having to ascend to the platforms. To account for the awkward site, Lewis designed a curving ticket hall with a setting-down area for cars. The original design featured a slim tower similar to Boston Manor and a parade of shops. These were both removed by Curtis post-war. The small ticket hall interior features a curved information display unit and exposed concrete beams to form the ceiling. A sweeping staircase with cream faience-clad walls and a bronze stair rail leads up to the platforms. The platforms themselves are rather exposed, with the main original feature here being the timber benches in the passenger shelters.

Station building: 1947

Designed by: Brian Lewis and FCC Curtis

Listed: Grade II

PERIVALE STATION
PERIVALE STATION

GREENFORD

Greenford opened on 30 June 1947, even though the station building was not finished. A temporary entrance was used as the rest of the station was constructed around it. The finished station is similar to Perivale, featuring a ticket hall with a curved facade abutting a railway viaduct. Unlike Perivale, the ticket hall at Greenford is one storey, with roof lights to illuminate the interior. The building is constructed of concrete, tiled at the lower levels, board-marked higher up. Until 2014 the station had the last wooden escalator on the network, which was also the first escalator installed for the Underground to take passengers up to the platforms rather than down.

Station building: 1947

Designed by: Brian Lewis and FCC Curtis

GREENFORD STATION
GREENFORD STATION

NORTHOLT

Northolt had had a halt-style station since 1907, but with the extension of the Central Line to Ruislip in 1948, a new modern building was needed. Unfortunately for Northolt, a lack of funding meant it didn't get one until the early 1960s. FCC Curtis, along with his assistants Howard Cavanagh and RH Jones, drew up plans in 1947, while a temporary building was being used. Their design had a rectangular ticket hall with a strip of windows and a wide entrance onto the street. By the time there was enough money to build the station, a simpler plan was felt to be a better fit, and John Kennett and Roy Turner produced the more austere building we see today.

Station building: 1948–61

Designed by: FCC Curtis, John Kennett and Roy Turner

NORTHOLT STATION
UNDERGROUND
CONSIDERATE

SOUTH RUISLIP

One of the most interesting stations on the tube network, South Ruislip can be seen as a transition from the Holden era towards a distinctive post-war style. Curtis used the circular plan of stations such as Southgate and Hanger Lane, with a substantial ticket hall space in reinforced concrete, lit by windows made up of 12 vertical strips each. This idea was revised in the final design by Kennett and Turner, who used translucent glass instead, giving the building an appearance of being clad in steel. Inside the ticket hall, a concrete frieze by artist Henry Haig runs around the interior. It is an abstract design inset with blue tiles and said to depict the busy rhythms of the station's day.

Station building: 1948–61

Designed by: FCC Curtis, John Kennett and Roy Turner

UNDERGROUND
OVERHEIGHT
VEHICLE
TURN BACK
LOW
BRIDGE
SOUTH RUISLIP STATION

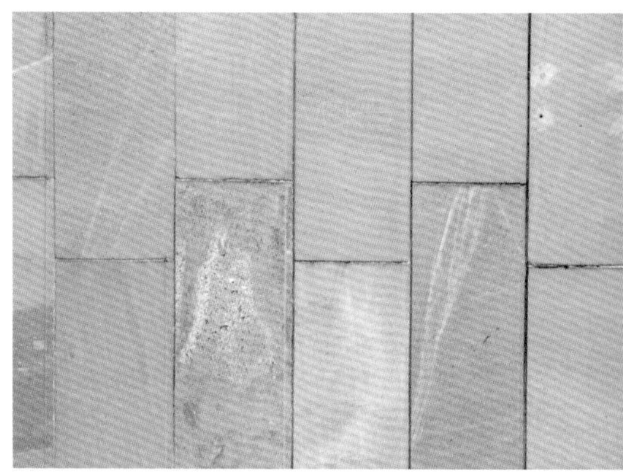

RUISLIP GARDENS

As built, Ruislip Gardens is the least interesting of the stations on the section of the Central Line. Had the original design of Frederick Curtis and his assistants been followed, it would have been a post-war take on the Holden 'Sudbury Box'. The ticket hall would have had windows facing east and west, but not onto the front of the station, and a parade of shops on either side. This idea was very much scaled down by Kennett and Turner, with just a single-storey ticket hall, faced at the front with slate and a roundel on a mast. The station did have a concrete butterfly canopy on the platform area added in 1949, but this was unfortunately demolished in 1998.

Station building: 1948

Designed by: FCC Curtis, John Kennett and Roy Turner

RUISLIP GARDENS STATION
UNDERGROUND

WEST RUISLIP

The terminus of the western extension once again opened in 1948 but wasn't finished until 1960. As at the previous three stations, Frederick Curtis produced the original designs, which John Kennett and Roy Turner amended. The differences between the original and finished designs are not as significant as elsewhere, with the size of the ticket hall being reduced. Built in white and yellow concrete brick around a portal frame, the ticket hall has a splayed concrete canopy at the front, incorporating a parade of shops in the established London Underground manner. The reinforced concrete passenger footbridge also recalls the work of Stanley Heaps in the 1930s, which zig-zag down to the platform areas.

Station building: 1948–60

Designed by: FCC Curtis, John Kennett and Roy Turner

WEST RUISLIP STATION

UNDERGROUND
55 BROADWAY
ST. JAMES'S PARK STATION
55 BROADWAY
55 BROADWAY
BROADWAY
UNDERGROUND
FREE

UNDERGROUND
WESTMINSTER STATION
THEATRE
UNDERGROUND
FREQUENT
ELECTRIC
TRAINS TO
ALL PARTS
OF LONDON

VICTIMS OF PROGRESS : DEMOLISHED STATIONS

Although this book is primarily concerned with the surviving works of Charles Holden and others for London Transport during the same period, several stations of the era weren't so lucky and have since been demolished. However, as is often the case with railway stations that have been operational for 100-plus years, individual elements may have been upgraded, rebuilt and altered separately, resulting in a patchwork of different architectural periods. The following few pages cover those primarily lost, though some Holden-era details may still be found in some instances.

Holden's first project for the UERL, as it was then, was two new entrances for Westminster station (1922–4). The first entrance, onto Bridge Street, was a simple canopy and doorway. The second, replacing a previous entrance on Thameside would set the scene for his Underground design work for the next 15 years. A plain rendered facade decorated with a roundel and bar logo replaced the previously gloomy doorway. Light, simple and modern, it represented the first step in dragging the tube out of the Edwardian era. The station was completely rebuilt to designs by Hopkins Architects in 1999 as part of the Jubilee Line extension.

Holden's next projects for the network were facelifting several stations that made up the City and South London Railway, later part of the Northern Line. Angel, Borough, Elephant & Castle, Old Street, Oval, Stockwell and Clapham North were all given new street-level facades and updated signage in 1924. Holden developed three different facade schemes for these stations, all composed of similar units depending on their existing shape. Light brown faience tiling was used as the main facing, with black faience edging. New branding was employed with the diamond motif and the 'UNDERGROUND' signs used for the first time. The interior of the new entrances was not handled by Holden but by the in-house engineering department. In some ways, Holden was using similar ideas to Leslie Green, the architect of the distinctive oxblood tile stations of the 1900s. But whereas Green used a standard building plan, Holden's varied according to location. All the Holden designs have been replaced by newer stations, although some elements remain at Angel and Clapham North.

Westminster Station, 1924

Previous pages: 55 Broadway and St. James's Park station

Further entrance redesigns followed at several sites in central London. Bond Street (1926), Post Office (now St. Paul's) (1929), Mansion House (1930) and Marble Arch (1932) all had new entrances and ticket halls designed by Holden. He used a similar palette of materials and arrangements as seen at the Morden extension stations of 1926, screen facades in Portland stone with large first-floor windows featuring a coloured roundel. A surviving example of this central London application of the aesthetic can be seen at Holborn (1933). Marble Arch differed slightly from the others in having ironwork louvres in place of a window. All four stations were redeveloped between 1979 and 1991.

Archway had opened in 1907 as the northern terminal of the Charing Cross, Euston & Hampstead Railway. In 1932, the station facilities were upgraded with escalators installed and a new entrance, designed by Holden, added onto Junction Road. This was an almost all-glass three-storey design with a small roundel sign. Holden also redesigned the platform decoration adding cream tiles with the station name in black. At this time, the station was called Highgate. In 1939 it was renamed Archway (Highgate), before becoming Highgate (Archway) in 1941, and finally just Archway in 1947! The above-ground station buildings were demolished in 1963 to make way for Archway Tower, which now sits above the station.

The extension of the Piccadilly Line westwards and its replacement of former District Railway services were the impetus for a few other station rebuilds that have subsequently disappeared. Hammersmith (1932) was reconstructed with new platforms added and the internal space redesigned. Holden also added a new entrance on Queen Caroline Street, which resembled the street entrance at Archway, albeit with a more prominent roundel. In the 1990s, the above-ground buildings were demolished to be replaced by a shopping centre that now acts as the entrance for the station.

Back towards the centre of London, three stations had improvements made to accommodate the increased traffic from the Piccadilly Line extension. Hyde Park Corner (1932) had a new ticket hall, and additional entrances were added to the 1906 Leslie Green station. The ticket hall featured the glass timetable and fare displays units also seen at Manor House. The above-ground station buildings were sold off and are now a hotel.

Top: Knightsbridge station, 1934; Borough station, 1924
Bottom: Clapham North station, 1924; Post Office station, 1929

UNDERGROUND
UNDERGROUND
UNDERGROUND
KNIGHTSBRIDGE STATION

UNDERGROUND
BOROUGH STATION
BOROUGH
TOBACCO
CIGARETTES
BOROUGH
DRY CLEANERS

UNDERGROUND
CLAPHAM NORTH STATION
CLAPHAM NORTH STATION
CLAPHAM NORTH STATION

POST OFFICE STATION
UNDERGROUND
POST OFFICE STATION

Originally opened in 1906 as Dover Street, Green Park was rebuilt and renamed in 1933. Holden designed a new subterranean ticket hall with a circular rooflight and a new southern entrance constructed in Portland stone with two large Underground roundels alerting passengers as to the station's presence. The station was redeveloped for the opening of Victoria Line services in 1969, with Holden's entrance being rebuilt and the ticket hall extended, and again for the Jubilee Line extension of 1999. Knightsbridge was another Green station from 1906 that needed rebuilding for the new Piccadilly Line traffic. A new entrance and ticket hall were built on the corner of Hans Crescent to accommodate the increased footfall, first opening in July 1934. Again constructed of Portland stone, and featuring the metalwork louvres seen at Marble Arch, Holden's work here was demolished in 2004 as part of an ongoing renovation of the station facilities.

Another station that has been redeveloped in the 21st century is Stratford. Now a major interchange station, with Central, District, Jubilee, DLR, Overground and Crossrail services, Stratford has grown out of all recognition from when the new Central Line ticket hall was opened in 1946. The building was designed by HH Powell, architect to British Railways Eastern Region, and its facade can still be seen, now standing forlornly in an empty lot. The design has similarities to the ticket hall at Mile End, with a cream tile finish, but unlike Mile End, it has no windows.

Hammersmith station, 1932

HAMMERSMITH
UNDERGROUND
SANDEMAN'S PORT
VICTORIA
CHEF
KETCHUP
GHOSTS
OLIVER LODGE
ROVINCIA • BANK
UNDERGROUND
UNDERGROUND
HAMMERSMITH

INDEX OF STATIONS

55 BROADWAY 40, 47, 48, 49, 188
ACTON TOWN 66, 67
ALDGATE EAST 126, 127
ALPERTON 68, 69
ARNOS GROVE 80, 90, 91
ARSENAL 50, 51
BALHAM 28, 29
BECONTREE 101
BETHNAL GREEN 148, 149
BOROUGH 193
BOSTON MANOR 76, 77
BOUNDS GREEN 88, 89
CHISWICK PARK 64, 65
CLAPHAM COMMON 24, 25
CLAPHAM NORTH 193
CLAPHAM SOUTH 26, 27
COCKFOSTERS 13, 21, 96 ,97
COLLIERS WOOD 34, 35
DAGENHAM EAST 102, 103
DAGENHAM HEATHWAY 101
DOLLIS HILL 140, 141
EALING COMMON 60, 61
EARL'S COURT 124, 125
EAST FINCHLEY 122, 123
EASTCOTE 116, 117
ELM PARK 104, 105
FINCHLEY ROAD 136, 137
GANTS HILL 158, 159
GRANGE HILL 162, 163
GREENFORD 178, 179
HAINAULT 165
HAMMERSMITH 195
HANGER LANE 174, 175
HARROW ON THE HILL 128, 129
HOLBORN 54, 55
HORNCHURCH 101
HOUNSLOW WEST 62, 63
KILBURN 130, 138, 139
KNIGHTSBRIDGE 193
LEICESTER SQUARE 56, 57
LEYTON 165
LEYTONSTONE 152, 153
LIVERPOOL STREET 146, 147
LOUGHTON 9, 166, 167
MANOR HOUSE 82, 83
MILE END 150, 151
MORDEN 38, 39
NEWBURY PARK 9, 144, 160, 161
NORTHFIELDS 4, 58, 74, 75
NORTHOLT 180, 181
OAKWOOD 9, 94 ,95
OSTERLEY 78, 79
PARK ROYAL 7, 110, 111
PERIVALE 176, 177
PICCADILLY CIRCUS 44, 45
POST OFFICE 193
QUEENSBURY 142, 143
RAYNERS LANE 114, 115
REDBRIDGE 156, 157
RODING VALLEY 165
RUISLIP GARDENS 184, 185
RUISLIP MANOR 118, 119
SOUTH HARROW 112, 113
SOUTH RUISLIP 182, 183
SOUTH WIMBLEDON 36, 37
SOUTH WOODFORD 165
SOUTHGATE 17, 92 ,93
ST. JAMES'S PARK 40, 46, 47, 48, 189
ST. JOHN'S WOOD 20, 132, 133
STOCKWELL 10
SUDBURY HILL 72, 73
SUDBURY TOWN 70, 71
SWISS COTTAGE 134, 135
TOOTING BEC 22, 30, 31
TOOTING BROADWAY 32, 33
TURNPIKE LANE 84, 85
UPMINSTER BRIDGE 106, 107
UPNEY 101
UXBRIDGE 108, 120, 121
WANSTEAD 154, 155
WARREN STREET 52, 53
WEST ACTON 168, 172, 173
WEST KENSINGTON 42, 43
WEST RUISLIP 186, 187
WESTMINSTER 190
WHITE CITY 170, 171
WOOD GREEN 86, 87

Train at dawn near Becontree

BIBLIOGRAPHY

Cherry, Bridget, Pevsner, Nikolaus *Buildings of England: London: North*
Yale University Press, 2002

Cherry, Bridget, Pevsner, Nikolaus *Buildings of England: London 3: North West*
Yale University Press, 1991

Cherry, Bridget, Pevsner, Nikolaus *Buildings of England: London 2: South*
Yale University Press, 1983

Croome, Desmond F *The Piccadilly Line: An Illustrated History*
Capital Transport Publishing, 1998

Croome, Desmond F, Graeme Bruce, J *The Central Line: An Illustrated History*
Capital Transport Publishing, 2006

Horne, Mike *The District Line: An Illustrated History*
Capital Transport Publishing, 2006

Karol, Eitan *Charles Holden: Architect*
Shaun Tyas, 2007

Lawrence, David *Bright Underground Spaces: The Railway Stations of Charles Holden*
Capital Transport Publishing, 2008

Leboff, David *London Underground Stations*
Ian Allan Publishing, 1994

Menear, Laurence *London's Underground Stations: A Social and Architectural Study*
Midas Books, 1983

Ovenden, Mark *London Underground By Design*
Penguin, 2013

Pevsner, Nikolaus *An Outline of European Architecture*
Pelican, 1963

Rose, Douglas *The London Underground: A Diagrammatic History*
Douglas Rose, 1980

Websites:
Oxford Dictionary of National Biography www.oxforddnb.com
Survey of London https://surveyoflondon.org
Heritage Gateway www.heritagegateway.org.uk/Gateway

BIOGRAPHIES

Philip Butler is a Worcestershire-based photographer focusing primarily on documenting the remains of Great Britain's inter-war architecture.
2019 saw the publication of Philip's book *Odeon Relics - Nineteen-Thirties Icons in the Twenty-First Century*, an annotated series documenting the surviving buildings constructed by the iconic cinema chain in the 1930s. www.philipbutlerphotography.com

Joshua Abbott is a historian, tour guide and photographer based in Welwyn Garden City. His Modernism in Metroland website and social media feeds have been cataloguing and celebrating Greater London's Modernist architecture for over ten years.
In 2020 his debut book *A Guide to Modernism in MetroLand* was published by the Unbound imprint. www.modernism-in-metroland.co.uk

First published by Art Deco Magpie in 2022.
This edition published in 2023.

FUEL Design & Publishing
33 Fournier Street
London E1 6QE

fuel-design.com

Design by Murray & Sorrell FUEL

Distribution by Thames & Hudson / D. A. P.
ISBN: 978-1-7398878-2-7
Printed in China

THOMAS LORD
55 BROADWAY